Bureaucracy, Organisational
Behaviour, and Development

Bureaucracy, Organisational Behaviour, and Development

PRAYAG MEHTA

SAGE Publications
New Delhi • Newbury Park • London

Copyright © Prayag Mehta, 1989

First published in 1989 by

Sage Publications India Pvt Ltd
M-32 Greater Kailash Market I
New Delhi 110 048

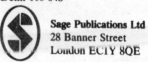

Sage Publications Inc
2111 West Hillcrest Drive
Newbury Park, California 91320

Sage Publications Ltd
28 Banner Street
London EC1Y 8QE

Published by Tejeshwar Singh for Sage Publications India Pvt Ltd, phototypeset by Mudra Typesetters, Pondicherry and printed at Chaman Offset Printers.

Library of Congress Cataloging-in-Publication Data

Mehta, Prayag, 1926–
    Bureaucracy, organisational behaviour, and development / Prayag Mehta.
    p.   cm.

    Bibliography: p.
    Includes index.
    1. Bureaucracy—India.   2. India—Economic policy—1947–
3. Organizational behavior.   I. Title.

JQ224.M44   1989   354.54'01—dc20   89–33179

ISBN 0–8039–9614–4 (U.S.)
      81–7036–156–7 (India)

To
Sushila, Pratibha and Vibhuti
They kept me going

Contents

List of Tables

List of Figures

Acknowledgements

This work owes much to many people and institutions. First of all thanks are due to senior officials of various central government departments who spared time for interviews, and the various administrative training institutes, state and central government officials who willingly participated in the study and provided data for it. Thanks are also due to Shri C.S. Tibrewal for his help in data collection, Shri B.S. Nagi, Senior Research Fellow, Council for Social Development, for his help in data processing, Dr. D.U.M. Rao for his help in preparing the index, and Shri Satya Prakash and Miss Suman Lata for their help in processing and typing earlier drafts of the manuscript. Special help was provided by Shri Jagdish Singh by repeatedly typing the manuscript in various phases of its preparation. Furthermore, I am obliged to the University of Delhi and its Faculty of Management Studies for their support for the research conducted for the present book. Last but not the least, thanks are due to several friends and colleagues who have provided comments on the earlier draft resulting in considerable improvement in the manuscript. The author alone is, however, responsible for any gaps or shortcomings which might have been left in the work.

1

Development Strategy and Performance in India

The central purpose of planning in India, as repeatedly stressed, has been to initiate a process of development in order to raise standards of living and open out new opportunities for the people. This has been guided by four main objectives: growth; modernisation; self-reliance; and social justice.

Large-scale pauperisation and backwardness of villages in India has continued to evoke a debate about the approach to development in the Indian context. On following the models of import substitution and industrial growth formulated by P.C. Mahalanobis and others, India forged ahead towards the development of a heavy machine sector and faster industrial growth. The public sector was recognised as the engine of growth and it soon scaled commanding heights in the economy. Also, within the agricultural sector new technology and infrastructural facilities have been used to stimulate greater production. As a result of this strategy the economy has been modernised in certain sectors; self-reliance has been achieved in several consumer goods, food production has increased greatly leading to self-sufficiency; and industry has become capable of producing capital goods like steel, cement, fertiliser, oil etc.

Growth Helps the Rich

The rate of growth in national income between 1950–51 and 1978–79 was reported at 3.5 per cent with the growth rate of 2.7 per cent in agricultural production and 6.1 per cent in industrial production. In per capita terms, income grew at the rate of 1.3 per cent with a 1.1 per cent per annum rise in per capita consumption. It (i.e., per capita consumption) grew by 46 per cent over the period between 1950–51 and 1978–79 (Planning Commission, 1980, Sixth Plan 1980–85: 1–5). However, the growth in industrial and agricultural production and an increase in national income does not help the poor. Improved technology and seeds promote agricultural productivity directly enhancing income from land. People who own land manage to increase their wealth without yielding any direct benefit to the landless agricultural labourers. In fact, the number of poor households increased from 30 per cent to 35 per cent during the period (1961–71) of intensive agricultural development (Sixth Plan 1980–85: 8). As the Draft Sixth Plan (1978–83) mentioned, the 'pace of industrialisation has not been bought cheaply. The concentration of economic power has increased in the sense that within the corporate sector, assets of bigger corporations have increased more rapidly.' It went on to add that under the influence of market economy and demand 'an unduly large share of resources is absorbed in production which relates directly to maintaining or improving the living standards of higher income groups' (Planning Commission, 1978: 1).

Approach to Agricultural and Rural Development

Various approaches have been adopted and specially designed programmes have been implemented in order to boost agricultural and rural development during the past several Five-Year Plans. These include zamindari abolition and land reforms; community development and introduction of Panchayati Raj institutions; intensive agricultural development based on improved technology and high yielding seeds; special schemes pertaining to the development of small and marginal farmers and landless agricultural labourers; common area development; drought prone area development; and integrated rural development.

Abolition of Zamindari and Land Reforms

Land reforms included abolition of land tenures like zamindaries, jagirdaries, etc., which covered some 40 per cent of the country s area. A small number of big absentee landlords, absentee money-lenders and the topmost section of landlords have been dispossessed of their land with payment of compensation. As a result of such measures a class of relatively small landlords, rich farmers, and a small section of upper-middle class peasants has emerged who have also become traders and creditors. Land ceiling legislation sought to determine ceilings on land and to bring about a re-distribution of surplus land among the landless and marginal land holders. However, studies have repeatedly shown that land continues to be concentrated in the hands of a few. The Sixth Plan (1980–85) reported that in 1976–77, 73 per cent of the rural people had either no land or possessed less than two hectares and operated only 23.5 per cent of all land. The remaining 27 per cent owned 76.5 per cent of the land, of whom 24.4 per cent were intermediate category farmers, possessing two to ten hectares of land and owning 50.2 per cent of the total area. Interestingly, 3 per cent households owned more than one-fourth of the total land, each one possessing more than ten hectares (Planning Commission, 1980: 8).

Community Development and Intensive Agricultural Development

Community Development was launched with great fanfare during the First Five-Year Plan itself. It was based on the assumption that village people could be motivated by extension and other admini-strative services. Huge funds were spent to provide infrastructural amenities like roads etc. Depending on the strategy of 'betting on the strong' (Wertheim, 1969: 894–902), more resources were diverted towards increasing agricultural output and far less to social and cultural amenities under the influence of western—primarily American—experts. As things worked out, there was a tendency to favour not only wealthier residents within a village but also wealthier villages and regions (Myrdal, 1968: 134). As was bound to happen, this resulted in the concentration of rural assets in the hands of a few rich and neo-rich peasants (FAO, 1980). No wonder it failed to enthuse the people and generate a self-sustaining base for development, as was stated in the plan.

Intensive Agricultural Development

New technology oriented intensive agriculture resulting in the 'Green Revolution' was implemented mostly in areas where the water supply was adequate and where farmers had sufficient resources to invest in such ventures. While use of biochemical and other technological innovations helped in raising food production considerably, the poverty situation did not improve (UNRISD, 1974; UNDP [FAO], 1979; FAO, 1980). The eventual improvement that was to come to the masses would have taken a long time in 'trickling down,' if indeed it ever would (Lele & Mellor, 1972; Mellor, 1976). Subsequently, the Sixth Plan came to the conclusion that 'programmes over the years achieved their objectives only partially. The bottom deciles of the rural poor, i.e., landless and the rural artisans, who are poorest, have in most cases been left untouched' (Planning Commission, 1980: 169).

Increasing Landlessness and Poverty

Studies indicate that over the period of intensified agricultural development and 'Green Revolution' the number of agricultural labourers in the country increased from 19.7 per cent to 26.3 per cent over two decades (i.e., 1951–71). It was clear that a large number of peasants lost their land and were pushed down the socio-economic ladder into the class of landless agricultural labourers. Furthermore, studies of the rural labour force revealed that the number of agricultural workers increased from 31.53 million in 1964–65 to 54.6 million in 1974–75. Both employment and rural earnings declined during the same period. Therefore, it was no wonder that a large number of rural people fell below the poverty line. As per Sixth Plan studies, about 51 per cent of the rural people were living below the poverty line in 1977–78 (Planning Commission, 1980: 7).

To sum up, one may say that post-independence measures and strategies employed to promote agricultural and rural development and to reshuffle the class configuration in rural India have, in fact, broadened the base of the proprietary classes comprising landlords and rich peasants who have been induced to increase production for maximising profits. At the same time, the process of proletarianisation and pauperisation has steadily accelerated (Desai, 1986: 23–24).

Integrated Rural Development Programme (IRDP)

As mentioned above, various evaluation studies conducted at the end of the Fifth Five-Year Plan concluded that development strategies were not successful in achieving their stated goal of poverty alleviation. It was found that the SFDA (Small Farmers Development Agency), which was designed to correct the situation by helping farmers with new seeds, improved technology, extension, credit, etc., and to help them in terms of supplementary income through dairy, animal husbandary, etc., was not really successful. The coverage was found inadequate; the provision was more of current inputs rather than additional inputs and the class of landless labourers was not reached. Thus, the conclusion for such special schemes was almost the same as in the case of earlier strategies. Summarising the assessment of India's economic development over a quarter century of planning, the Draft Sixth Plan (1978–83) put it succinctly:

> We must face the fact that most of the objectives of Planning have not been achieved, the most cherised goals seems to be almost as distant today as when we set out on the road to planned development. The aims implicit in all our plans, but more explicitly stated in later formulations of our development strategy, are universally accepted by the Indian people: they are the achievement of full employment, the eradication of poverty and the creation of a more equal society (Planning Commission, 1978: 2).

The Draft Sixth Plan, therefore, sought to alter the development strategy. The growth model and the 'trickle down' theory were given up in favour of a 'direct attack' on poverty. It visualised a total development plan for a block within which specific beneficiary schemes were set up. The Sixth Plan (1980–85) reviewed the functioning of various schemes during 1978–79 and came to the conclusion that 'constraints from which these programmes suffered have not been financial but organisational inadequacy and lack of a clear-cut plan of development and the area to which coordinated efforts of all concerned agencies can be directed.' Therefore, it recommended the replacement of multiple agencies by an integrated programme and called it the Integrated Rural Development Programme (IRDP). It was stated that the 'IRDP has been conceived essentially as an anti-poverty programme' (Planning Commission, 1980: 171).

PERFORMANCE IN RURAL AND SOCIAL DEVELOPMENT

The IRDP

The IRDP was extended to cover all the 5011 development blocks in the country by 2 October 1982. Since then several intensive case studies and extensive sample surveys have been conducted to assess the performance of this 'direct attack' programme. One such case study of Kerwara block of Udaipur district of Rajasthan provides some insight into its functioning. During 1982–83, 80 per cent of the households were supplied with a bullock and bullock-cart. Out of the total subsidy of Rs. 29.20 lakhs for agricultural development under IRDP, 90 per cent of the amount was spent on these two items. Reports that the same bullock and same cart were shown against several households indicate the extent of mal-practice in this connection. Another case study of Gulbarga and Udipi *talukas* in Gulbarga district of Karnataka emphasises that the IRDP schemes were mainly utilised by people living above the poverty line and furthermore it took about a year for the benefits to reach the beneficiaries after the scheme was approved (Jain *et al.*, 1985).

The National Bank for Agricultural and Rural Development (NABARD) undertook an extensive survey to assess the functioning and impact of the programme, covering 30 districts, 60 blocks, 122 bank branches and a sample of 1498 beneficiaries spread over 15 states in the country. It was found that the number of families covered under the programme upto 1983–84 totalled about 12.57 million as against the physical target of 12 million with investment credit of Rs. 2244 crores. This was about 94 per cent of the financial target. The study, however, came to the conclusion that the 'quality and general impact left much to be desired' (NABARD, 1984: ii). The NABARD study confirmed the findings of the above mentioned case studies, namely, that the IRDP adopted a uniform strategy resulting in providing a dairy even in drought-prone districts. It also empahsised the need for assistance to individual beneficiaries except in a few cases, although the policy provided for a cluster approach. In some cases, officials insisted on providing loans etc., to individual tribals who were themselves reluctant to approach banks for credit as they had reservations about getting into debt. Excepting West Bengal, where identification of beneficiaries was done by the block staff jointly with the bank personnel, elsewhere it was done mostly by the block staff resulting in delays in sanctioing of credits etc.

The block staff put an over-emphasis on physical targets resulting in mis-classification. As much as 15 per cent beneficiary families did not belong to the poorest of poor category. In some places, as in Gujarat, such mis-classification was to the extent of 47 per cent. The cluster approach was not implemented seriously. The administration took for granted that all beneficiaries would have the skills to manage dairy assets. Little or no attention was paid to infrastructure. In many cases poor quality animals were supplied. Thus, it is no wonder that 25 per cent of the beneficiaries expressed dissatisfaction in this regard. There was a lack of supportive follow up. The banks suffered from staff shortages and the block staff did not provide support to the banks. It was found that in some 13 per cent cases, loans to the farm sector were mis-utilised and in another 40 per cent cases assets were sold off. In the Industries, Services and Business (ISB) sector the problem was more serious (NABARD, 1984: vi–xi).

In addition to the above NABARD study, several other evaluation studies of the IRDP (such as State Bank of Hyderabad, 1983; Punjab National Bank, 1984; Central Bank of India, 1982; Jain, 1983; Ahuja and Bhargava, 1984; Central Bank of India, 1983; Krishna, 1984; State Bank of Bikaner and Jaipur, 1984) confirmed the following facts about the administration of the IRDP:

1. Mis-classification of beneficiaries.
2. Beneficiaries wanting to avail of loans because of the subsidy accompanying it even when the selected activity was of no use to them.
3. Guidelines regarding age, breed, season of purchase etc., were not followed in the purchase of animals.
4. Infrastructural and support facilities such as fodder, veterinary and marketing facilities etc., were not satisfactory.
5. The recovery was hardly 25 per cent and some of the beneficiaries thought that the loans would be written off as it was a gift from government.

Thus, the conclusion reached by NABARD that the quality and

general impact of IRDP left much to be desired was confirmed in many other studies conducted across the country. Both intensive case studies of blocks and districts and surveys, clearly indicated several policy and administrative lapses in implementation of the programme. 'The failure to assess the specific beneficiary oriented scheme against the availability of needed resources in the area, their possible use by others than the poor, the commitment for the product in the market, etc., before persuading targeted members to accept loans and subsidies have led to widespread wastage and failures' (Rath, 1985: 234). It has been estimated that in at least 4000 out of 5011 blocks in the country, the IRDP has been equated with 'cow and buffalo' scheme (Subramanium, 1985).

Education

The people of India should have enjoyed free and universal elementary education by 1960, i.e., ten years after the promulgation of the Constitution. However, the progress of education has been very dismal. Out of 179 million children in the age group of 5–14 years—about 27 per cent of the total population in 1981—only 38.45 per cent of those in the age group of 5–9 years and some 50 per cent in the age group of 10–14 years were actually enrolled in schools. It was worse in rural areas where two in every three children in the age group of 5–9 years and six in every ten in the age group of 10–14 years were not attending school. Children of scheduled castes and scheduled tribes, and girls in general were the worst sufferers (Census, 1981).

Primary schools are marked by a high degree of infrastructural constraints. Of the total number of primary schools in the country, only 47 per cent were housed in permanent buildings, 59 per cent of the schools were without drinking water facility; 85 per cent without lavatory; 40 per cent without blackboards; 53 per cent without playgrounds and 71 per cent of the primary schools had no library facilities (Krishna Kumar, 1985). Under such conditions it was no wonder that more than seven out of every ten children enrolled drop out without completing their schooling (Ministry of Education, 1985: 36).

Child Labour

Majority of the country's 263 million children (in 1981) in the age group upto 14 years—about 40 per cent of the total population—

live and work in poverty. Of these, 5.46 per cent, about 14 million, are main workers, i.e., those working on a full time basis (Census, 1981). Some earlier estimates put this number at 17.36 million (Banerjee, 1979). We seem to contribute more than one-third of Asia's child labour and one-fourth of the world's working children (ILO, 1981). Mounting child labour is a standing testimony of our failure to fulfil the constitutional directive for the protection and education of children.

Malnutrition and Human Resource Development

Importance of the human factor in socio-economic development can hardly be over-emphasised. Lack of education and work creates a vicious circle which greatly reduces the quality of our human potential. Addressing the Indian Parliament in 1958, Gunnar Myrdal (1987) decried rigidity in planning and stressed the urgency of adequate nutrition and health to strengthen work and education. However, malnutrition among women and children has continued unabated over all the development years as a fatal consequence of poverty. Minimum income and purchasing power are essential for obtaining nutrition, health and education and therefore, the well-being of the family. Lack of minimum income makes it necessary for the family to withdraw children from schools and induct them into the labour market. As a consequence, we are faced with a very high rate of school drop-outs and wastage in education. Malnutrition of mothers and children has jeopardised our human resources. It has been estimated that out of 23 million children born in India during 1982–83, only three million would be able to grow as truly, healthy, physically fit, productive and intellectually capable citizens. Some nine million of them were likely to emerge into adulthood with impaired physical stamina and low productivity because of serious malnutrition and ill-health during their childhood. Another seven million might reach adulthood with less striking physical and mental impairment (Gopalan, 1983). Therefore, lack of proper nutrition has seriously impaired productivity, creativity and the working quality of our people, thus contributing to a process of de-humanisation.

Environmental Contamination

Along with increasing poverty, there has been a fast degradation of genetic resources and environmental contamination leading to widespread diseases. These factors have seriously affected the working capacity of the rural labour force. It is now common knowledge that forest resources have been destroyed in several parts of the country thus creating an ecological imbalance which in turn affects the lives of millions of people (Dasholi Gram Swaraj Mandal, 1982).

Drinking Water and Transport

The goal of the International Drinking Water and Sanitation Decade was to provide safe drinking water and sanitation to all by 1990. This is also essential for the fulfilment of our declared policy to provide health for all by 2000 A.D. However, reviews show that despite the water decade and the declared policy, fewer people have access to clean and adequate water than ever before (Sharma, 1985).

We suffer from a lack of adequate infrastructural facilities like transport, roads, irrigation, etc. However, more important is the fact that even these scarce resources are not necessarily properly maintained. There are frequent reports of these services going out of use through disrepair and for want of proper maintenance. It is estimated that some 36 per cent villages are not connected with roads and even in those villages which are some 70 per cent cannot be reached even on foot during the rainy season (Janak Singh, 1985). Not only are these very scarce and precious resources wasted, but such wastage and poor maintenance has a cyclic effect on the quality of life of the people.

Physical Indices of the Quality of Life

The quality of life is bound to be affected when the majority of the people are illiterate, most of whom are also without productive work and for whom basic amenities like nutrition, drinking water and health facilities are largely lacking. Such deprivations are reflected in the infant mortality rate (IMR) and life expectancy at age one which are important indicators of the quality of life. The poor performance in this respect is reflected in a high IMR and high death rate at 127 per thousand and 13.6 per thousand respectively as recorded in 1981, as against the targeted national goal of 60 and 9 respectively by the year 2000 A.D. Similarly, the birth rate of 32.6 per thousand and life expectancy at 51.6 years as recorded in 1981 were far behind the targeted goals respectively of 21 per thousand and 64 years by 2000 A.D. (*India Today*, 15 March 1984). It is instructive to compare our targets with those proposed by the Club of Rome as basic human needs, with a literacy rate of 77 per cent, IMR of 50 per thousand, and life expectancy at age one of 67.4 years by the year 2000 A.D. (Tinbergen, 1976). Thus, even if we succeed in achieving the targets set for the year 2000 A.D., we would be lagging behind the basic requirements of an adequate quality of life.

Development Goals in the Seventh Plan

Development goals projected by the Seventh Five-Year Plan (1985–90) need to be studied in the context of our performance during the previous plans. It continues to put emphasis on an improvement of the quality of life of people in India, particularly the poor. In this connection it has been envisaged that per capita consumption of foodgrains and cloth and per capita generation of electricity and generation of employment would go up considerably by 1990 and much further by the year 2000. As a result of such socio-economic development efforts, it is hoped that longevity of life would be enhanced to 58.6 years and 63.3 years for males and 59.7 and 54.7 years for females by 1990 and 2000 A.D. respectively. The infant mortality rate would go down to 90 per thousand by 1990 and further down to 60 by the year 2000 A.D. Correspondingly, the death rate would also come down substantially by these periods (Planning Commission, 1985, Table 2.11). It has, therefore, been emphasised that removal of poverty, promotion of higher productivity through modernisation, investment and planning, equipment and technology, promotion of skills and education of the labour force, necessary for new science and technology would be taken up at a much faster degree than ever before (Manmohan Singh in his preface to the Seventh Plan, 1985).

STATED GOALS AND ACTUAL ACHIEVEMENTS

Every successive plan in India, as we have seen in the foregoing analysis, has pledged to eradicate poverty and bring about greater equality among the different classes of people. Interestingly, reviews at the end of each plan more or less revealed that instead of achieving the stated goals, the opposite seemed to have happened. Instead of decreasing poverty and landlessness, economic development has strengthened the rural rich—landlords and rich peasants—as well as the urban rich—industrial monopolies, big entrepreneurs and educated elites.

The Factor of the Parallel Economy

The dismal performance in the nation's priority development areas seems to be correlated with the continuously expanding parallel economy and the emergence of the all powerful factor of black money. Conservative estimates suggest that such money has been multiplying at a terrific rate. In the early fifties such money in circulation was estimated at Rs. 400 crores (Kaldor, 1956). It increased to Rs. 1400 crores in 1968–69 (Govt. of India, DTEC Report, 1971). Some years later, i.e., 1983–84, it was estimated between Rs. 31,584 crores to Rs. 36,786 crores (or about 18 per cent to 21 per cent of the GDP at current prices (NIPFP, 1986).

One of the important sources of black money is the expansion of governmental expenditure over the years. Some twenty-five years ago the Santhanam Committee (Govt. of India, 1964: 10) recorded large-scale practice of payment of regular percentage to government officials as commission in construction contracts, purchases, sales and other regular business on behalf of the government. The NIPFP study (1986: 217) confirmed that 'leakages from public expenditure are a pervasive and not an isolated phenomenon. Experienced civil servants indicated that leakages from anti-poverty programmes (such as IRDP) in the range of 10 to 30 per cent are quite common, while in some cases they may be higher.'

Thus, black money has become an all pervasive and tremendously influencial factor in our socio-economic life. This great money power is used to create and finance pressure groups and organise lobbyists who in turn campaign for pro-rich policies. One of the serious consequences of this phenomenon is the concentration of wealth in fewer hands and the widening gap between the rich and the poor.

It is, therefore, not possible to judge government policies by stated goals and priorities alone. What is more important is the actual performance in various development areas. There is a difference, sometimes a split, between word and deed. As Griffin (1974: 172) has put it, 'rather than criticising governments for failing to attain what they did not set out to attain or offering advice on how to attain a non-goal, it would be instructive if more time were devoted to analysing what governments actually do and why.'

Bureaucracy and Development

We have briefly analysed the development achievements and health of the Indian economy to enable us to focus on the functioning and behaviour of the Indian bureaucracy in the development process. The term 'bureaucracy' has been used in preference to 'civil services' as the latter carries a restricted meaning associated with only the higher levels of public services whereas 'bureaucracy' includes all categories of government employees structured and arranged in various ways and levels, constituting public administration in the country.

The Seventh Plan has greatly emphasised the role of administration in development in terms of managing the infrastructure; speedy disposal of matters; and responsiveness to developmental needs. It has been envisaged that an effective administration would need coordination between different sectors of government including simplification of laws, rules and procedures. Therefore, planning itself should be increasingly associated with appropriate administrative arrangements and personnel policies, more specifically in the less developed and remote areas for implementation of programmes for the weaker sections. It is essential to emphasise the need for motivation and values in bureaucracy in accomplishing goals in economic and social development (Seventh Plan, 1985: 8).

Accordingly, the Plan has proposed a major thrust for human resource development. It has been emphasised that there must be

> substantial improvement in the quality of agricultural and rural development administration. Technical knowledge and skills of the officers at grassroot level of administration need to be greatly improved for imparting scientific temper to agriculture. Finally, we must bring about meaningful participation of people in national development (Manmohan Singh in his preface to the Seventh Plan, 1985).

Development Performance and Bureaucracy

The nature and role of the bureaucracy needs to be understood in the context of past development performance and the stated goals of development set for the country toward improving the quality of life of the people. As we have seen above actual achievements greatly depend on the general development strategy and the related policies as well as on the functioning of the administration. The Seventh Plan has stressed the role of the bureaucracy, its involvement in and commitment to various planned programmes such as employment generation, land reforms, equity in distribution, health care, water supply and sanitation and on raising the quality of these services for general improvement (Planning Commission, 1985: 47).

Bureaucracy has occupied an important position in India since British colonial rule. It became all the more important after independence. As we will see later, it has proliferated enormously and has got entrenched in all walks of life in the last few decades. It has become an integral and inseparable part of the developmental process. So much so that developmental performance has become almost synonymous with the performance of the bureaucracy. Therefore, it is no wonder that the planning authority repeatedly stress the need for gearing it for achieving the goals it has set before the country. However, an analysis of our developmental performance suggests that our bureaucracy has neither been 'goal-directed' nor 'action-oriented' as far as alleviation of poverty, promotion of social equity and social development of people are concerned. In subsequent chapters, we present and discuss some data regarding bureaucratic perceptions and attitudes at the higher levels and some aspects of organisation behaviour of the middle level bureaucracy in the country. Such data may help in explaining the development performance and the functioning of the government in managing development programmes and projects.

2

Bureaucracy in India

The erstwhile Indian Civil Service (ICS) was known as the 'steel-frame,' set up for protecting the interests of the colonial masters in India. Brilliant university graduates, trained in classical studies, Greek, Latin etc., were selected for the ICS. Not only was there no scope for specialisation in the service, it was, in fact, not appreciated (Macaulay's Report of 1884). It was designed as a powerful 'generalist' cadre to be always at the top of any other service or posting. Its superiority was very strictly guarded by the British. The officer was encouraged to tour areas under his jurisdiction akin to a feudal lord (Bhambhri, 1972). Almost total exclusiveness of the service and its distance from the people were promoted. Such values and practices were taught and reinforced.

Exclusiveness served the purpose of maintaining law and order and in perpetuating the oppressive rule. The officer was not at all accountable to the people whom he ruled. The bureaucracy ruled by instilling fear and awe in the people. Such emotions were used to intimidate large masses, and farmers in particular, to pay taxes and for other related revenue collection. Therefore, the civil service with the ICS at the top was designed, promoted and rigidly organised to serve British imperial goals of exploitation and subjugation of the people of India. Historical analysis of the evolution of bureaucracy in India shows that the dominant consideration behind its organisation and recruitment after 1858 was for the most part political (Mishra, 1977: 388).

The ICS and the Freedom Movement

The Indian freedom movement, therefore, kept a safe distance from civil servants particularly those belonging to the Indian Civil Service. They were perceived as being the lackeys of British imperialism. Congress Party leaders tried their best to keep them at bay lest the Congress 'left' took advantage. So much so that when the popular governments came to power after 1935, the Congress ministries kept the officers of the Indian Civil Service away and made attempts to develop a parallel administration outside the existing structure (Mishra, 1977: 395).

In his autobiography, which was written during the independence struggle, Jawaharlal Nehru emphasised that national development in India was not possible without demolishing the Indian Civil Service and the values embodied in the services. He wrote that 'no new order can be built up in India so long as the spirit of the ICS pervades our administration and public service' (Nehru, 1953: 282). It was clear that the Indian people and the national movement greatly decried the attitudes, values and bureaucratic practices as symbolised in the Indian Civil Service and perceived them as impediments to national freedom and development.

Values Expected of Public Servants

The freedom movement projected new values and motives which public servants were expected to adopt to help build a new India. These were naturally diametrically opposed to the colonial anti-people values of the ICS and the bureaucracy nurtured by the British in India. Gandhiji gave a dictum in this respect to guide and set the tone of bureaucratic behaviour. He laid down his famous ground test for the public services as follows:

> I will give you a talisman. Whenever you are in doubt or when the self become too much with you, apply the following test. Recall the face of the poorest and the weakest man whom you may have seen, and ask yourself, if the step you contemplate is going to be of any use to him. Will he gain anything by it? Will it restore him a control over his own life and destiny? In other words, will it lead to Swaraja for the hungry and spiritually starving millions. Then you will find your doubt and yourself melting away (quoted in Haldipur, 1984: 98).

Thus, Gandhiji explicitly made the bureaucracy accountable to the people and their needs. He called upon the elite to become sensitive and responsive to the needs of the poorest of the poor, thereby imbibing values of social responsibility. In his scheme of values, duties were more important than powers. He greatly emphasised austerity, simplicity, discipline, hard work, sense of social and personal responsibility and selfless devotion to the cause of the poor. He also stressed the empowerment of the people as an important goal for the civil servants, so that they help the poor person regain 'control over his life and destiny'. He particularly stressed the need for participatory, socially sensitive and responsive bureaucracy which greatly valued service to the people. Some years later Gunnar Myrdal (1987: 21) recalled these values to the members of Indian Parliament. While addressing them on 22 April 1958, he decried that such values as taught by the Father of the Nation were not adhered to in Indian planning and administration.

Continuation of the ICS after Independence

The reactions of the ICS at the dawn of independence were expectedly mixed. One group was ready to happily change over to the 'Gandhi cap' and to resort to simple living and adjust their habits accordingly. Their reaction in this respect reflected the prevailing mood (e.g., simple living) as nurtured by the freedom movement. Another group assessed that the pivot of British parliamentary institutions was the civil service and that political bosses may come and go without making much difference. In short, they felt that the 'steel-frame' character of the administration should be retained intact (Durga Das, 1969).

However, despite its strong denunciation by national leaders, particularly Jawaharlal Nehru, the ICS continued to exist after independence and withered away only when the last of the ICS retired in 1980. Even after retirement, several of them continued to wield great influence in the government as governors, advisors, chairmen of autonomous bodies etc.

Indian Administrative Service and Other Civil Services

The Indian Administrative Service (IAS) was formed soon after independence. Gradually State Administrative Services and several other all India and central and state civil services and cadres came into existence. The IAS took over the functions of the ICS. Its authorised strength was 3203 on 1 January 1971 which had increased to 5047 by 1 January 1984. The authorised strength of the other two all-India services, namely, the Indian Police Service (IPS) and the Indian Forest Service (IFS), also grew during this period. Their authorised strength, respectively was 1790 and 1097 in 1971 and 2679 and 2006 in 1984. The total number of civil personnel under the central government (excluding Union Territories) rose from 17.37 lakhs in 1956 to 37.87 lakhs as on 1.1.1984. The growth of personnel under state governments was still larger. While the number of civil employees under the central government increased from 28.4 lakhs in 1971 to 32.9 lakhs in 1983, in the various states it increased from 42.2 lakhs to 63.3 lakhs during the same preiod, representing an increase of 16 per cent and 43 per cent respectively. Most of the state employees belong to organised services (Third Central Pay Commission Report, 1973, Vol.I; Fourth Central Pay Commission, Report, 1986, Part I).

Of the central government employees, about 40 lakhs, nearly 71 per cent were blue collar workers in 1984 and the rest were white collar employees. In the latter category, 7 per cent were administrative personnel; 9.9 per cent were technical and professional (engineers, doctors, scientists etc.) and 18.5 per cent were clerical/ supervisory personnel (Fourth Pay Commission, 1986).

Thus, along with an increase in development programmes and other activities, the bureaucracy also has greatly proliferated mostly at middle and lower levels. The self-proliferation power of the bureaucracy follows an interesting process. One of the essential elements in project formulation and its implementation is the creation of additional posts. This tendency is an inherent characteristic of the regulatory system which leads to a growth in 'establishment' work (Murthy, 1984). Thus, over the years since independence a gigantic bureaucracy has grown at centre, state, district, block and village levels. It is rigidly hierarchical in nature and quite differentiated in its work. Such characteristics are found to exist irrespective of the fact whether bureaucrats work in regulatory or developmental department (Jain and Chaudhuri, 1982).

It is this sprawling bureaucracy which is entrusted with the task of formulating and implementing development programmes and other activities. Therefore, the civil services have been playing a crucial role in meeting the growing developmental needs of independent India. Attention has been, therefore, focused on administrative services from time to time to examine their functioning and to see how they have been discharging their developmental functions. Some earlier studies called attention to the Indian social structure dominated by tradition bound institutions like caste, colonialism, sectarianism, regionalism, etc., which set the tone of group behaviour (Shils, 1962). Such Weberian characteristics of bureaucracy as 'objective discharge of business according to calculable rules and without regard to person' (Gerth and Mills, 1948: 215) were therefore, not likely to operate under such social conditions.

Values Inherited from the ICS

However, studies also suggested that control oriented regulatory system of administration inherited from British colonial days has little value for development administration in underdeveloped countries where a need was for an adaptive administration, one that could incorporate constant change (Thompson, 1964: 21). Several studies conducted in the early 1960s on Asian bureaucractic system and the influence of British imperial traditions clearly show that British values continued to set the tone of bureaucracy in India and that there was no radical departure in the behaviour from pre-independence norms (Braibanti, 1966).

Gandhi's dictum of serving the poor was seldom found in practice. Instead, studies conducted in the 1970s to examine the specific response of the Indian Administrative Service to change found that many of them were development oriented. However, their commitment to modernising change and people's aspirations was rather low. Concentration of power in the hands of generalist administrators at the district level made them authoritarian and isolated them from the mainstream of masses (Bansal, 1974). Bureaucratic considerations were characterised by status-consciousness. This was clearly reflected in the personality of the higher level bureaucrats as seen in their day-to-day behaviour. The system was heavily inclined towards routine administrative tasks and the concentration of authority suggested strong power orientation unsuitable for achievement of goals (Singhi, 1974).

Interface with Panchayat Raj and People

In the wake of the community development programme, came the institution of Panchayat Raj which spread fast in the country during 1960s. This changing situation brought the Indian bureaucracy face to face with the elected people's representative in the local self government at the district and block level. Studies conducted in this respect came to the conclusion that the existing administrative organisation which was developed for law and order and revenue collection and which has grown much bigger over the years was inadequate for achieving the goals of development. The system was not able to relate with elected people. They looked down on the emerging politicians, although they were ready to bargain with them (Chaturvedi, 1977; Mathur, 1972).

Continuation of Imperial Values and Attitudes

Not only were pro-people values and attitudes weak, but specifically designed studies found continuation of earlier imperial values and attitudes in Indian bureaucracy after independence. The culture of Indian bureaucracy was found in similar rules, regulations, procedures, control-mechanism and basic management practices as were followed in British days. It was found that the firmness, harshness and impersonality used by the British in holding subordinates down were in turn used by the same subordinates in their dealings with the villagers. This approach came to be known as the 'official' way of management which was in fact the product of the patronising approach of the colonial bureaucracy which was grounded in a sense of fear and awe by which farmers were made to pay taxes to the representatives of the extractive bureaucracy. Through a process of social learning the villagers formed an image of exploitative, extractive and hostile government workers. They naturally tended to transfer this image to extension and development workers also (Higgenbothem, 1975).

Studies, therefore, suggested that the Indian bureaucracy continued to maintain its rigid hierarchical structure with centralisation of power at higher levels and also, more or less, maintained its regulatory and 'dominative' character. It has not been able to incorporate the desired changes in its structure and behavioural orientations. On the contrary, bureaucratic organisations seem to be moved by old imperial values and the traditions of the ICS.

Concept of 'Committed' Bureaucracy

There was political awareness regarding the nature of the Indian bureaucracy and its dominant values and orientations. During the first split of the Congress party towards the end of the 1960s the role of the bureaucracy came in sharp focus and criticism. Two young 'turk' leaders of that period, namely, Chandra Shekhar and Mohan Dharia, in their note on Basic Economic Issues to the requisitioned meeting of the AICC, remarked that:

> The present bureaucracy under the orthodox and conservative leadership of ICS with its class prejudice can hardly expect to meet the requirements of social and economic change alongwith socialist line. Creation of administrative cadre committed to national objectives and responsive to our needs is an urgent necessity (Hindustan Times, 1 December 1969).

Later, in his address as the Congress President Jagjivan Ram also referred to a 'lack of commitment by bureaucracy in India' (Hindustan Times, 31 December 1969). The emerging political situation in the country led to a debate on the concept of a 'committed' bureaucracy and the need for such a bureaucracy for development in India.

During the same period, when the need for a 'committed' bureaucracy was being discussed and advocated, the government came out with several radical economic programmes. The commercial banks were nationalised and the privy-purses of the erstwhile princes were abolished. *garibi hatao* (abolish poverty) was projected as a powerful election slogan which got strong attention of the electorate (Mehta, 1975). Thus, apparent radicalisation of the socio-economic programme was accompanied by a call for radical change in the Indian bureaucracy.

The 'Expert' and General Base

During the same period, when the need for a 'committed' bureaucracy was being debated, the Administration Reforms Commission, working through various task forces and committees, was engaged in recommending changes in the structure and functioning of bureaucracy in India. The Deshmukh Committee on administrative arrangements and administrative machinery particularly emphasised the importance of inducting professionals and experts in the secretariat and other levels of the bureaucracy. They wanted close integration of experts with generalists in the administration in order to enhance the expert base of the Indian bureaucracy (ARC Committee, 1968). At about the same time the Fulton Committee in England emphasised the need for trained professionals in civil service. It came to the conclusion that:

> Technical progress and increasing amount of knowledge have made a major impact on administrative tasks and the related process of decision-making. Setting new aspirations, striking right balance between coal, gas, nuclear power, electricity and in new energy policy, all these problems compelled civil servants to use new knowledge, new technology of analyses and professional approach (Fulton, 1968: 10).

Reflecting the contemporary political climate, the Third Central Pay Commission reiterated the need for enhancing the technical base of the Indian bureaucracy. Discussing the expanding tasks, they said:

> The scope of government activities in the modern welfare state has expanded both extensively and intensively in recent years. With the advent of development planning, the role of scientists and technologists has assumed greater importance. The pay structure has to reflect such change in social values (Third Pay Commission, 1973: 28).

However, the above sentiment was only marginally reflected in pay scales recommended by the Commission. Quoting views of state governments and chief ministers, they justified continuation of higher pay scales for the IAS on the basis that they 'shoulder higher responsibility' than other services. While there was some attempt at bringing about parity between the 'general' and the 'technical' wings, the generalists, particularly the IAS, continued to dominate the bureaucracy. Despite the intended reforms, the IAS continued to persist in the image of the ICS with all its drawbacks. The power of the bureaucracy was greatly enhanced during the Emergency period of 1975–77, when the normal political process was derailed. The police power and the regulatory functions of maintaining 'law and order' clearly got the upper hand which further strengthened the generalist cadres in the bureaucracy. The services were allowed to restrict their intake, keep their monopoly over strategic positions in the bureaucracy and enjoy prerequisites like housing in exclusive posh areas in return for their political loyality (Blair, 1980; Hiro, 1976; Selbourne, 1977).

Development Inadequacy: Strengthening of General Bureaucracy

As mentioned earlier, the early 1970s were marked by some radical economic measures like nationalisation of banks and abolition of privy-purses. It was also during this period that *garibi hatao* programmes were announced. However, as mentioned in chapter 1, the Draft Sixth Plan (1978) came to the conclusion that the most cherished goals of poverty eradication and the creation of a more equal society remained almost as distant as before. Direct anti-poverty programmes like integrated rural development launched and implemented during 1980s, as discussed in chapter 1, also left much to be desired. Continuous inadequacy in development performance in terms of stated objectives should have led to a serious reexamination of administrative structures. Instead, we find continuous strengthening of the generalist cadres in the Indian bureaucracy during this period.

The Fourth Central Pay Commission (1986) reversed the thinking initiated towards the end of the 1960s for strengthening the expert and technical base of the bureaucracy and recognised the supremacy of 'generalist' cadres by attaching greater importance to the IAS and other all-India cadre of generalist administrators. The non-cadre officers including engineers, educationists, social scientists and other specialists were shown their place. Political commentators perceived such recommendations as evidence of the weakening of the parliamentary political system and the erosion of the authority and status of political functionaries including Union ministers, state chief ministers not to mention members of Parliament and state legislators. Such erosion has increased the dependence of political rulers on the higher echelons of the bureaucracy at the centre and states and has enhanced the latter's role in the governance of the country. The Fourth Pay Commission only paid obeisance to this undeniable fact of political life (editorial in *Economic and Political Weekly*, 5 July 1986).

Political Finance and Regulatory Functions

The emergence of the pre-eminent role of the bureaucracy in governance (or mis-governance) needs to be understood in the context of the increasing and all pervasive power of black money with its unfolding culture of kickbacks, cuts and commissions. Furthermore, the scope for making black income from government projects, programmes and purchases is far greater today, and a great deal of political finance is raised through such black income from government contracts, etc., 'with orders placed abroad being particularly lucrative propositions' (NIPFP, 1986: 19). It has been estimated (Pendse, 1983) that Rs. 170 crores of black money was spent on the 1980 Lok Sabha elections. Allowing for leakages en route, Rs. 400 crores of black income would have had to be generated to assure that Rs. 170 crores become available for actual election expenditure. Adding elections to state assemblies and various local bodies as well as inter-election requirements for political campaigning and manipulations, it is quite clear that the demand for political funds could easily average several hundred crores per year.

A World Bank report discussing the effects of corruption on administrative performance noted that corruption contributes to inter-ethnic and inter-regional conflict and violence. In addition, corruption undermines the legitimacy of political institutions and thus the government is less able to rely on the cooperation and support of the public. As a result, the government is compelled to resort to force and coercive tactics to maintain order. The resulting violence and political instability hinders political development (Gould and Amaro Rayes, 1983). Such conditions force the government to rely more and more on the regulatory and 'law and order' bureaucracy. The ascendancy of the Indian Administrative Service needs to be viewed in this political situation. The performance of government administration is bound to suffer under such conditions, thus retarding political as well as socio-economic development.

Participatory Administration and Human Resource Development

It is interesting, however, that the government has been repeatedly stressing the need for people's participation in development tasks and for participatory administration (Sixth Plan, 1980: 183; Seventh Plan, 1985: 8) and for promoting the organisation of rural workers to ensure that the intended benefits go to them (Sixth Plan, 1980: 407 and Seventh Plan, 1985: 5). Simultaneously, the need for human resource development and for the provision of professional support and expert services has also been emphasised.

Despite such reiterations and pronouncements, the government clearly opted for a strong 'generalist' thrust in administration thereby explicitly reviving the old colonial 'steel-frame' as reflected in the then ICS. This change was an important political development as it reflected the growing importance given to regulatory administration, maintenance of law and order, bureaucratic distance from people and an extremely elitist approach in the administration of the country.

However, the tasks on ground require experts, people's participation, high morale and motivation among civil servants, harmonious relationship between different cadres of the civil service as needed for the achievement of the stated objectives of development, particularly rural and social development. The supremacy of certain cadres within the civil service over others, particularly experts and specialists, tends to thwart such relationships and motivation.

Study of Organisational Behaviour

The emerging socio-economic and political situation, including increasing importance being attached to regulatory functions and to 'generalist' cadres in the bureaucracy, has been marked by a development process benefiting the rich much more than the poor. Such a situation is likely to shape the behaviour of the bureaucracy in various ways, particularly with regard to the formulation and implementation of development programmes. How do the senior bureaucrats working at the central level perceive the situation?

How do the middle and lower level civil servants working at state and district levels perceive the situation? What attitudes and motivation do they exhibit towards their work and work organisation? How do they tend to relate to social issues and to the prevailing political culture? We seek to analyse and provide answers to such questions in the following chapters.

3

Government's Senior Management, Politics and Development

The Constitution describes the all-India services as services which are common to the centre and the states. The IAS, IPS and the Indian Forest Service are all-India services created under the enabling provision of Section 263 of the G.O.I Act, 1955 and by virtue of Article 312(2) of the Constitution. These were created by the Parliament. The All-India Services Act, 1951 empowers the central government to make rules etc., for these services in consultation with state governments (Fourth Pay Commission, 1986: 109–22). The concepts underlying the all-India services as given by the Administrative Reforms Commission are as follows: common recruitment which should ensure a uniform standard of education, language of the states and availability of experience gained in different parts of the country.

Central Staffing Scheme

The scheme of staffing administrative posts at the centre was introduced from the year 1957. The scheme covers all posts of and above the rank of under secretary in the Government of India. The personnel are drawn from all-India Services, Central Group 'A' service, officers belonging to several other central and state services. The normal tenure of deputation is three years for under secretaries, four years for deputy secretaries,five years for joint secretaries/directors and above with a provision that in case a person of joint secretary rank is promoted as additional secretary, the tenure should be three years at the level of additional secretary.

40 BUREAUCRACY, ORGANISATIONAL BEHAVIOUR & DEVELOPMENT

Central Secretariat

Secretaries of the ministries and departments of the Government of India together constitute its headquarters organisation. The number of secretariat departments was 18 in 1947, 25 in 1957, 51 in 1973 and 71 in 1985. In the administrative hierarchy of the central government, the secretary occupies a key position and his main role is to help the government in tasks of policy formulation, to prepare programmes in order to translate policies into coordinated action and to ensure effective execution of government policies through periodic reviews. The secretary also helps the minister discharge his accountability to Parliament including various parliamentary committees (Third Pay Commission, 1973: 86).

The central secretariat of the Government of India was manned by 878 officers of the rank of deputy secretary and above in 1984. Of these 378, or 43 per cent, belonged to the IAS. The remaining posts were held by members belonging to several other services including Indian Audit and Accounts Service (IA&AS), Indian Revenue Service (IRS), Indian Police Service (IPS), Indian Railway Accounts Service (IRAS), Central Secretariat Secretary (CSS) and others. The post of joint secretary is the lowest level taken as belonging to the senior management class by the Administrative Reforms Commission. The joint secretary in charge of a particular wing is expected to function more or less as a secretary, submitting papers directly to the minister from whom the orders emanate but pays regard to the secretary who is generally responsible for the functioning of the ministry as a whole. The importance of the IAS can be understood by the fact that out of the total of 192 joint secretaries in 1984, 135 (i.e., 70.3 per cent) belonged to the IAS. There were 61 secretaries and 66 additional secretaries of whom 36 (or 59 per cent) and 27 (or 41 per cent) respectively belonged to the IAS (Fourth Pay Commission: 114).

Therefore, the IAS has emerged as the most influential of the civil services. The IAS officers occupied most, i.e., 62 per cent, of the senior management posts at the headquarters of the Government of India in 1984. However, roughly 75 per cent of the IAS officers work in various states and rest on deputation to other posts including those in the Government of India. By virtue of their position, the IAS officers occupy the most dominant management role in the central government as well as in various state governments.

Personal Interviews

It was decided to conduct personal interviews with a small sample of senior IAS officers working at the headquarters of the Government of India. Sixty such officers were picked at random from departments such as Health, Education, Food and Civil Supplies, Agriculture and Rural Development, Finance, Personnel, Labour, Home Affairs, Works and Housing, and Environment. Some 35 of them agreed to give time for the study. However, only 21 of them were eventually available for the detailed interview in connection with the present study. The interviews were conducted during April–June 1985 at New Delhi. The respondents were secretaries, additional secretaries and joint secretaries to the Government of India. Each interview was a detailed exercise with questions, probes and further probes designed to obtain a variety of perceptual data and opinions of the senior bureaucrats manning the top management in the country. As mentioned in chapter 2, the interviews were directed to obtain perceptual data regarding certain important and desired aspects of the administrative structure; organisation behaviour of the Indian bureaucracy including morale and motivation of officers and employees; and development behaviour concerning goals, performance and desired achievement. The obtained responses were content-analysed and processed appropriately. These are reported and discussed below.

THE PERCEIVED ADMINISTRATIVE SCENE

Enhancing the Participatory Base

Indian Five-Year Plans have repeatedly emphasised the need for people's participation in management of public affairs designed to quicken nation-building and development tasks. It has been repeatedly stressed that 'in ultimate analysis the objective of removal of poverty can be fulfilled in the measure in which the poor themselves become conscious, improve their education and capabilities and become organised to assert themselves.' It was also mentioned as one of the objectives of the Sixth Plan. The need for workers' participation underlined for the rural development process. The role of government agencies was to 'help people to help themselves'. It was pointed out that the success of programmes designed to achieve rapid development in the quality of life of the rural and urban poor 'will depend upon the extent of involvement of our vast human resources in national development' (Planning Commission, 1980: 183).

The Seventh Plan (1985–90) further stressed the need for an interaction of people's participation with public administration for effective programme implementation and for streamlining the administrative machinery in this respect (Approach Paper, 1985: 5). At the global level, United Nations agencies have been stressing an interface between social and economic development, their mutual reinforcement and the importance of popular participation and local decision-making in this regard (United Nations, 1980: 6).

As was expected, a large majority, 86 per cent, of the senior bureaucrats interviewed for the present study stressed the importance of people's participation. At the same time, they were quite aware that it has not been put into practice as seen in Table 3.1. Their perceptions implied at least some dissonance between the 'desired' national policy objective on one hand, and actual achievement in this regard on the other. Needless to say that in the absence of people's participation., programme formulation and implementation remained entirely in hands of the bureaucracy, with predictable consequences.

Table 3.1
*Top Bureaucratic Perceptions Regarding
People's Participation*
(N = 21)

Items	Responses (in per cent)	
Participation of people important in development programmes	Yes 86	Doubtful/No 14
Extent to which people's participation presently exists	Just Moderate 20	Low/None 80
Aware about ILO Convention 141 (ratified by the Govt. of India) regarding organisation of rural workers	Aware 43	Not Aware 57

Measures for Improving People's Participation

The senior officials suggested several ways and means of improving people's participation in developmental efforts. Their responses provide an inkling of their attitude towards this oft stressed objective of planning in India. Their responses revealed the following: (a) people's participation had, over the years, been 'politicised' with political parties trying to promote the participation of their 'loyalists' only and excluding others opposed to them. This has also resulted in greater 'political interference' at the district level which in turn has not only weakened the administration but also prevented people's participation from becoming a reality. Therefore, it was suggested that offices of deputy commissioners or collectors' at the district level should be made the nodal agency thus enabling them to mediate between the people and government. They should be provided with funds which in turn would be sanctioned to voluntary agencies in order to promote people's participation; (b) some of them emphasised the need for the extension of education and training for the target groups as well as civil servants in order to sensitise and prepare the district level officials for promoting people's participation; (c) there was a feeling that 'participation' has been grabbed by the 'haves' as a consequence of which the 'have-nots' have been left out of the process. Both voluntary agencies and the district administration should be strengthened for promoting people's participation.

Thus, as could be expected, senior bureaucrats, like various government agencies, talked about the need for people's participation. Some of them went a step further and expressed dissatisfaction with the phenomenon of the 'rich' taking undue advantage of participatory forums. Their misgivings about political parties was, however, interesting. They saw them as an 'interference' and voluntary agencies as a 'supporter' in this respect. They talked only in terms of bureaucratic interventions for promoting people's participation. In their scheme the leadership remained in the hands of the bureaucracy rather than with political institutions.

Organisation of Rural Workers

The attitude among senior bureaucrats came out more sharply as they talked about the organisation of rural workers—the 'have-nots' about whom they spoke of earlier. After reviewing past experience, the Sixth Five-Year Plan took a step further in defining the need for participation of the rural poor in the developmental process. It recalled that the Government of India had ratified the ILO Convention 141 (ILO, 1982) which 'enjoins that it shall be the objective of the national policy concerning rural development to facilitate the establishment and growth of strong and independent organisations of rural workers'. The Plan, therefore, underlined the importance of involvement of rural workers' organisations as essential for 'ensuring the benefit intended for rural workers under the various development porgrammes'. Noting further that it would take time for the voluntary agencies and trade unions to make a dent among these sections, it was therefore 'necessary for the state machinery to facilitate the process in the initial stages' (Planning Commission, 1980: 407). The Seventh Plan proposes to further strengthen the programme of the organisation of rural workers. The plan stressed that in the ultimate analysis, the objective of removal of poverty can be fulfilled in the measure in which the poor themselves become conscious, improve their education and capabilities and become organised and assert themselves (Planning Commission, 1985: 5).

Therefore it was only reasonable to expect that senior bureaucrats would at least be aware of this important national policy. However, when asked about it, as many as 57 per cent of them were found to be unaware of this Convention and the subsequent policy. Their lack of awareness, and unconcern in this respect highlighted the nature of bureaucratic interest in rural workers and for the policy as well.

Their attitudes came out more clearly on further probing. All of them, irrespective of whether they knew about the policy or not, were asked to give their views about the policy of the organisation of rural workers. Most of them displayed a negative attitude to the policy, for the following reasons: (a) organisation of rural workers would only hamper the growth of the economy as was the case with the organised sector. According to them, trade unions were holding the country to ransom; collective bargaining was 'funny'; that these (trade unions) make politicians more important, and encourage laziness and indiscipline among workers and employees. Some of them gave the example of the state of Kerala where

workers were highly organised as a consequence of which indus-
trialists were moving away to the neighbouring states; (b) the
organisations of rural workers cannot remain politically neutral.
The programme would, therefore, lead to more political conflicts;
(c) even programmes like minimum wages soon become law and
order problems. Promotion of organisations of rural workers
would further add to this situation; (d) involvement of officials in
promoting such organisations would spoil their 'neutrality'; (e) it
was difficult to organise industrial workers and it would be much
more so to organise rural workers; (f) such a programme would
heighten caste differences and conflicts which in turn would result
in greater divisions in rural society.

There were a few officials who supported the policy of organising
rural workers. They suggested the following in promoting this
programme: (a) reorientation of civil servants through training
and education to make them more sensitive and responsive to the
needs of the poor; (b) the programme should be taken up on a
priority basis and proper funds should be made available to
promote such organisations; (c) the question of organising rural
workers is linked with the larger question of land reforms. It was,
therefore, essential that political parties should become more
active in this connection; (d) more voluntary agencies should be
encouraged to get involved in this programme, as bureaucrats
themselves would not be able to do much in this respect; (e) adult
education and literacy programme should be encouraged on a
larger scale in order to promote consciousness among the rural
workers and to promote their organisation.

Concern for 'Professional Neutrality': Political Behaviour of the Bureaucracy

One common thought discernable in the numerous responses,
irrespective of whether they opposed or favoured the policy for
promoting the organisation of rural workers, was their disdain for
political parties and fondness for 'neutrality' of civil servants
between various sections of the rural society. There was an
apprehension that law and order problems which were likely to
emerge when rural workers get organised might threaten their
'neutrality'. Many years ago, Jawaharlal Nehru discussed this issue
of neutrality of civil servants and said that

in a period of dynamic growth we want people with minds, people with visions, people with desires to achieve, who have some initiative to hold the job and who can think about it; but a person who is completely neutral is a head clerk (without any disrespect) and no more. He would do his work efficiently as head clerk no doubt but nothing more. Can a person be neutral, I ask you, about the basic needs for which our State stands for . . . . (IIPA, Speeches of Nehru, 1975: 75.)

After four decades of independence and despite the national policy to promote organised participation of the people, the top echelons within the bureaucracy continue to clamour for 'neutrality'. This betrayed their class affiliation. Their behaviour implied their need to side with landowners and the propertied class who wield great influence over the State apparatus. As a senior bureaucrat remarked elsewhere,

it is well known that significant segments of the bureaucracy have a class bias as they have a direct linkage with the rural elite. Though undesirable it is understandable that such a bureaucracy would have an additional block against any radical land reform. But even where the bulk of the bureaucracy comes from the urban middle class with no land linkage, it behaves the same way. (Bandyapadhayay, 1986: A 56)

Their mistrust and contempt of 'politicians' and an over-emphasis on neutrality, in fact, revealed their political behaviour. No wonder the landed class manage to divert resources and benefits to themselves, even those which are earmarked in the 'policy' for the poor. It was an interesting theatrical situation where, on one hand, the senior bureaucracy is involved in formulating a policy and on the other, the same bureaucracy is clearly hostile to its implementation. The actual policy on the ground, therefore, becomes an anti-thesis of the 'stated' policy with clear advantage to the entrenched vested interests.

Staff Participation in Decision-Making and Management in Government

Like the organisation and participation of rural workers, the

Government of India has been repeatedly talking about workers' participation in management of industry (Ministry of Labour, 1975, 1977, 1983). A similar need has been stressed from time to time in respect of participation of lower levels of the bureaucracy in decision-making and management within the government. Drawing attention to the contribution of small technicians to the industrial revolution, Nehru asked the senior civil servants:

> Do we ever consult or make efforts to get ideas from the people lower down on the scale of administrative apparatus? Do we care to know what they think about their work . . . that has a double purpose in view. One is that we might get good suggestions particularly from persons who are actually doing the job. Secondly, that you will make them have a sense of partnership much more than they do at present . . . (IIPA, 1975: 61.)

The Administrative Reforms Commission and the various Five-Year Plans have been reiterating the need for such participation in government decision-making and for their greater involvement in the management of public affairs. The Seventh Five-Year Plan has stressed such a need with its thrust on human resource development (Planning Commission, Seventh Plan, preface, 1985). It was, therefore, significant (as seen in Table 3.2) that seven out of ten

Table 3.2
*Perceptions Regarding Staff Participation
and Usefulness of Associations*
(N = 21)

Items	Response (in per cent)	
Practice of staff participation in management and decision-making in government	*Would improve functioning of public administration* 30	*May worsen functioning of public administration* 70
Do staff associations and trade unions help in promoting staff participation?	*Yes, they serve a useful purpose* 33	*No, they are harmful and dysfunctional* 67
Do employees themselves want to participate?	*Yes* 29	*Doubtful/No* 71

29

respondents were opposed to such a management practice. Their reasons were the following: (a) employees are interested only in their service and working conditions. They work only for money and the system is plagued by corruption; (b) decision-making in government is not the same as in industry where there is ownership both in private and public sector; (c) there is already a system of joint consultative machinery (JCM). Further staff participation in government decision-making would only confuse issues and create problems.

Staff Associations and Trade Unions

It is noteworthy that as many as 312 federations, unions and staff associations gave oral evidence before the Fourth Central Pay Commission. They belonged to various departments and ministries of the Government of India including associations of all-India services, i.e., IAS, IPS and Indian Forest Service (Fourth Pay Commission, 1986: 35–43). Thus, staff associations and employees' unions have increasingly become a widespread phenomena in the government. They represent different interest groups in the Indian bureaucracy. Their dislike of trade unions and staff associations should, therefore, be viewed in this context.

Further investigation regarding staff associations and trade unions and their role in administration brought out sharp attitudes and opinions. Most of them, i.e., two-thirds, believed such bodies to be harmful and dysfunctional. Reasons given in this regard were: (a) associations and unions raise demands in their self-interest which only retard the overall development of the country; (b) leaders have ulterior motives and politicians take undue advantage of such bodies and create conflicts within the administration.

A minority, i.e., one-third of them, viewed staff associations positively. Active associations could help in generating development thinking from bottom upwards which was lacking in the present situation. There were, however, mixed feelings as they also apprehended the assertion of self-interest by associations which could release divisive forces in the government. Some of them believed, rather strongly, that staff participation would loosen the present rigid hierarchy in government bureaucracy, smoothen government functioning and work as a controlling mechanism on the authoritarian functioning of senior officials which goes against the best interests of the people. Thus, it could democratise the administration and bring it closer to the people.

Do Employees Want to Participate?

A majority of senior officials—seven out of ten—believed that employees themselves did not want to participate in government decision-making as they were interested only in bargaining for personal interests. They were interested in their rights rather than in improving the functioning of the administration. Some who viewed it favourably, saw the need for training and education in this regard. However, they also believed that the present administrative system was not geared to promote such participatory practices and that the system itself would have to be reformed.

Thus, despite repeated talk of the need for people's participation, the organisation of the rural poor, and staff participation, the top bureaucracy sees a threat to law and order and to their 'neutrality' from such declared policies. Furthermore, they visualise political interference and apprehend the ascendance of trade unionism which they would like to exclude and instead may like voluntary agencies to help implement programmes including people's participation, albeit under their control. They look down upon the inclusion of lower levels of the bureaucracy with decision-making processes and consider it impractical. Such attitudes at the apex level of the civil service, reinforced by a weakening of political institutions (as discussed in chapter 2), tend to revive and perpetuate the 'steel-frame' administrative apparatus. However, as seen in chapter 2, widespread corruption generates administrative inefficiency and ineffectiveness. Under these conditions, such attitudes at the top would create an atmosphere of mistrust at all levels of public administration.

Development of Subordinates

In a situation of increasing complexity regarding developmental and administrative tasks, senior bureaucrats can play an important role in helping their subordinates learn new skills and develop their capabilities. However, because of corruption the 'top administrators are discouraged from training their subordinates to undertake increased responsibilities, while their ability to supervise is also reduced' (Gould and Amaro-Reyes, 1983). Therefore, it was not surprising to find that senior officials in the present study could hardly recall any experience of preparing and developing their subordinates, as can be seen from Table 3.3. Lack of such helping behaviour assumed greater importance in view of seniors' perception that the employees in general lacked expertise and preparedness for handling expanding developmental tasks.

Table 3.3
Perceived Expertise and Preparedness in Civil Servants in General, and Superiors' Role in Developing Subordinates
(N = 21)

Items	Response (in per cent)	
Expertise and preparedness of the employees in general for handling expanding jobs	*Competent, Prepared*	*Not sure of competence or/and not prepared*
	14	86
Recall experience of preparing/ developing subordinates	*Able to recall such experience*	*Not able to recall*
	24	76
Conflicts among development programmes	*Yes*	*No*
	50	50

The increasing need for expertise and preparedness in civil services was stressed during further investigation. They made the following suggestions in this regard: (*a*) training and education; (*b*) adequate working and service conditions and incentives in general; (*c*) sound transfer policy and inter-change between secretarial and field postings and an adequate wage policy for development officials at the district level as poor wages tended to corrupt them; (*d*) adequate support system in terms of technical knowledge and expertise for development officials; (*e*) personal involvement of senior bureaucrats in developing their subordinates and functionaries at the lower levels, team functioning to inculcate a feeling of partnership and joint functioning in various projects and reorientation of senior officials as well as political executives in order to help develop subordinates and to promote in them a concern for development.

The senior officials also believed that a helping relationship and the task of developing subordinates were not easy under the present administrative system and culture. They traced the source of poor expertise and low preparedness to this system. A few of them did perceive their role in developing team work and expertise for an improved functioning of the government.

Harmony and Conflict in Development Programmes and Goals

Pursuing the matter further regarding some important aspects of administrative structure in the country, senior officials were asked to comment on the prevailing state of harmony among various development programmes and goals. Orchestration is obviously necessary for achieving the overall developmental goal of poverty alleviation and nation-building. This was all the more important in view of the proliferation of development programmes over the years with corresponding proliferation of personnel, agencies and departments.

The Planning Commission and various related government departments have repeatedly been emphasising the need for coordination among various agencies in order to obtain the harmonious implementation of programmes. Commenting on this situation, 53 per cent of senior officials interviewed clearly perceived a lack of harmony in this respect. Some of them thought that instead of producing harmony, the conflicting departments produced 'cacophony' with resultant consequences. Interestingly, they blamed the political culture for this situation also. However, the politicians were not willing to take responsibility for failures. They claimed that some departments did not want to know what other departments were doing so that they could continue to implement programmes in their own way. As a consequence, they held the senior bureaucracy responsible for this situation.

Analysing it further, some of them raised a counter question: 'who is interested in coordinated management of programmes? Nobody.' Bureaucratic and political apathy, strong emphasis on financial and physical targets, allegiance of personnel to their own departments and groups, lack of coordination—all worked in favour of powerful vested interests who manage to divert benefits and funds to themselves thus leaving the poor to fend for themselves. The system, on the whole, was insensitive and non-responsive to the needs of the people. This was the real problem implicit in the lack of harmony in various development departments and programmes.

PERCEIVED ORGANISATIONAL BEHAVIOUR

Perceptual data, as presented above, brought out some important behavioural orientations obtaining at senior levels of the bureaucracy. Implicitly as well as explicitly they revealed a dislike and distrust of politicians and trade unions; apprehended increasing conflicts in rural areas viewing them as law and order problems, and visualised staff indiscipline and incompetence in case of decentralisation and democratisation of decision-making. There was also some kind of dissociation between their 'desirable' and actual behaviour. For instance, senior bureaucrats 'talked' of the need for coordination, professional expertise and preparedness among their subordinates, people's participation and decentralisation. However, they seemed to 'act' in an uncoordinated manner, did little to develop their subordinates and delegate powers to them and also did little to promote people's participation and organisations. They also talked about the inefficiency of the present rigid system of administration. However, not only did they do little to change it, but acted to strengthen it in all possible ways. The responses, therefore, threw light on the nature of the administrative organisation as well as on the senior bureaucrats organisation and political behaviour.

Morale, Motivation and Concern for Development

The senior officials also provided interesting information on certain pertinent dimensions of general bureaucratic behaviour. They spoke about morale, motivation, concern for development, work satisfaction and also of making the government work faster. They further analysed and identified related factors existing in socio-political, organisational and working conditions. Their thoughts in this regard are briefly summarised below.

Employee Morale

Employee morale, obviously an important factor for effective development administration, was perceived to be low, as can be seen from Table 3.4. Linking the problem of low morale with several important structural variables, they considered the following factors as responsible: (*a*) unsatisfactory working and service conditions. This was the most important factor associated with an unfair transfer policy, poor pay scales, lack of facilities for family and children in rural areas, unfair promotion and reward policy particularly for those working in the field; (*b*) too much external interference; (*c*) development programmes, by and large, have themselves become routine and stereotyped; (*d*) growing tendency among employees to attach greater importance to their own income, i.e., their own self-interest, rather than the interest of society. This was both a manifestation and a cause of the problem; (*e*) there was a growing tendency towards sycophancy among senior officials which percolates down in the system contributing to demoralisation.

Table 3.4
Perceptions Regarding Job Satisfaction, Morale and Motivation

Items	Response (in per cent)	
Rating of Job Satisfaction among Officers in General	*Moderate to high*	*Doubtful to low*
	57	43
Rating of Work Satisfaction among Employees in General	29	71
Rating of Morale of Civil Servants in General	*Moderate to high*	*Low to very low*
	35	65
Rating of Concern and Motivation for Development Programmes	09	91

On further investigation, several suggestions emerged for restoring and promoting morale among the bureaucracy. These included promoting job challenge in order to satisfy social and psychological needs of the employees; promoting team work and a sense of togetherness for common goals; clarity in policies and goals; close interaction between superiors and subordinates in a non-hierarchical manner and support to the latter in order to improve their authority, i.e., decentralisation. There was a need to reduce 'officialdom' for raising bureaucratic morale. Thus, senior bureaucrats once again saw the need for de-bureaucratisation and organisational re-designing for enhancing civil servants' morale for development tasks. They talked about it, analysed it further and freely offered suggestions for improving the situation. These suggested practices were, however, conspicuously absent in their administrative behaviour.

Concern and Motivation for Development

The concern for development—particularly for the poor—among civil servants is obviously an important factor in motivating programme-implementation for the achievement of 'stated' objectives. In a striking perception top managers rated such concern for development as low to very low (Table 3.4). Coupled with the emphasis on self-interest such behaviour indicated widespread bureaucratic alienation from people and goals of development, particularly in regard to programmes of poverty alleviation, equality and social justice.

Reasons for Low Concern for Development

Analysing the problem, senior officials gave the following reasons for such low concern: (a) poor working and service conditions particularly at district and field levels. This was the most important; (b) general lack of infrastructure and supportive services for programmes like rural development, education, health etc.; (c) political culture of interference, poor leadership—both bureaucratic and political—cumbersome and confusing instructions and guidelines; (d) in-built tendency to support the rich, resulting in advancing huge loans, sometimes running into crores of rupees, to them, and a strong hesitation in advancing small loans even of Rs. 5,000 to the poor despite instructions and policy; (e) lack of effective local self-government; (f) traditions of looking at the administration as *huzur mai bap* (paternal lords).

How to Improve Concern for Development

Suggesting ways of improving the situation, they once again stressed the following: training and education; seniors' support to subordinates; fair policy of reward and punishment; adequate service and working conditions; decentralisation; technical support to civil servants; and better management system for development programmes.

As the seniors' role was repeatedly stressed, respondents were requested to recall (from their own working experience) instances of such help and support to their own subordinates. Only five out of twenty-one senior officials could recall some such experience. Further probes also could not evoke much response. This indicated that the ideas being suggested remained merely at the verbal level, mostly as pious desires without a corresponding effort to put them into practice. As one of them remarked, it was an example of 'officialdom' and passing the buck. Thus, interaction, close human touch, rapport with subordinates, team work, spirit of togetherness etc., remained only as good slogans without corresponding determination for practising them. Implicitly, this was symptomatic of some kind of bureaucratic schizophrenia—split between 'saying' and 'doing,' between 'verbal' and 'actual' behaviour. Such a situation at the top was bound to affect the morale and seriousness at other levels of the bureaucracy, thus affecting the functioning of the government as a whole.

Work Satisfaction

Work satisfaction is an important factor in efficient functioning of any work organisation, and governmental organisations are no exception. How much satisfaction do officials and employees derive from their work? How much motivation do they have for doing their jobs well in order to achieve organisational goals including important developmental goals as envisaged in various plans and programmes? The assessment of senior bureaucrats can be seen from Table 3.4. On the whole, they rated work satisfaction as low among officers and much lower among employees in general. A majority of the lower grade employees and a large number of upper grade personnel were perceived to be dissatisfied with their work/jobs. It becomes all the more serious when viewed in the context of the proliferation of the bureaucracy in the country with obvious implications for governmental functioning and implementation of development programmes.

Factors Responsible for Officers' Low Work Satisfaction

Analysing it further, several reasons were offered for low work satisfaction which fell in three broad categories, namely: (a) socio-political conditions; (b) the nature of the work/job itself; (c) working, living and service conditions including salary. The prevailing political culture topped the list of dissatisfiers for the officers. Such conditions included: (a) political interference in appointments, postings, transfers, promotions, decision-making, etc.; (b) over-staffing; (c) feudal attitudes bred by the social system are carried into the workplace resulting in victimisation, particularly at the district level; (d) increasing social tension and violence and the resultant sense of insecurity among officers.

Interestingly, one-third of the responding senior bureaucrats perceived the nature of the job itself as the reason for low work satisfaction. On the one hand their expertise is not fully utilised, and on the other they are compelled to do certain things which they did not consider useful. There was also a feeling that they were on jobs not by choice but because there was no alternative. At times, their jobs are dull, repetitive and meaningless. One-fourth of them also considered living and working conditions including salary as inadequate. Additionally, as a result of growing staff indiscipline, there was a feeling of insecurity and tension.

Table 3.5
Factors Responsible for Low Work Satisfaction

Items	Per cent of total responses	
	Officers	Staff Employees
Socio-political conditions	42	22
Nature of the job/work itself	33	17
Working, living and service conditions including salary	25	61
Number of Responses	**12**	**18**

Factors in Employees' Low Work Satisfaction

The order of the factors was reversed in case of lower grade personnel. For them, poor working, living and service conditions including salary were perceived as the most important factor. As many as 61 per cent of them believed that they were working under adverse conditions and that their pay scales were not attractive. Some personnel, like village level workers, are forced to stay on the same position for more than twenty years without any promotional avenues. The prevailing political culture also made its contribution to this dissatisfying work scenario.

It was, thus, interesting that senior officials saw much greater dissatisfaction with the prevailing political culture at higher levels and with working and service conditions at lower levels. Such conditions of life and work greatly influenced the work and developmental behaviour of the bureaucracy. It was interesting to note that the same factors (such as the political culture) did not affect the entire bureaucracy in the same way. Different layers and groups within it reacted and behaved varyingly depending probably on their specific situation.

Making the Government Work Faster

Soon after the new government headed by Rajiv Gandhi took office in January 1985, public discussion was initiated for reforming governmental functioning. Proverbial red-tapism, the tendency to pass the buck, sitting on files and delaying decisions, excessive adherence to rules and rigidity have been repeatedly criticised as factors responsible for low efficiency. As mentioned above, interviews for the present study were conducted during April–June 1985, the period when such issues were being debated. They were asked (in the interview) to give their assessment of the probability of the success of such efforts.

Half of them, nearly 52 per cent, perceived moderate to high probability of success in efforts designed to reduce red-tape and enhance flexibility and promptness in governmental functioning. The remaining half were pessimistic in this regard. The findings assumed greater importance in view of their timing. It should be recalled here that one of the promises made by Indira Gandhi during the 1980 elections was to provide a 'government that works'

(AICC [I], 1979). The promise made by Rajiv Gandhi in 1985 was to give a 'government that works faster' (AICC [I], 1984). There was a heightened level of expectation among the people as the new government under youthful leadership took over following the massive mandate. Thus, at the height of such euphoria, a sizeable section of the concerned bureaucracy was sceptical of such efforts.

On further investigation, the 'sceptical' officials remarked that the matter was not that simple. It needed a detailed analysis and radical restructuring of the administration. There were all kinds of checks, controls, and blocks like audit, parliamentary and constitutional provisions including administrative laws, regulations etc., which slowed the functioning of the government. An official could be taken to a court of law for a wrong decision even several years after. Even a bonafide mistake could be used for witch-hunting. They believed that the prevailing corruption in the system, accompanied by the harassment of the public, is correlated with slow decision-making in government. The British colonial system which was based on mistrust has continued to function in independent India. It means an increasing accountability of officers but without corresponding trust and powers. The system did not promote an informal relationship of mutual trust between superiors and subordinates which alone could pave the way for faster decision-making. In fact, the present system promotes the opposite. In absence of a proper analysis, action planning and strong political will to reform the administrative structure, it was doubtful whether the government could be made to work faster.

Thus, senior officials envisioned low morale, very low concern for development and people, and moderate to low work satisfaction in the Indian bureaucracy, particularly at middle and lower levels. They regarded the prevailing political culture, the existing system of administration and job design, poor service and working conditions, poor political and bureaucratic leadership as important factors shaping such organisation behaviour. Attention was, therefore, needed to deal with such structural and organisation factors for enhancing motivation, boosting morale and concern for development, enhancing job satisfaction, and for toning the organisations. In the absence of such analysis and action, it would be difficult to make the government work faster and still more difficult to make it work for the poor and for poverty alleviation.

DEVELOPMENT PERFORMANCE

Formulation, coordination and implementation of development plans greatly depend on the public administrative system and its bureaucracy. The Planning Commission, Administrative Reforms Commission and several other public institutions have repeatedly stressed the need for restructuring the administration. It was, therefore, not at all surprising that the same was repeatedly stressed by senior officials who were interviewed for the present study. The importance of enhancing and strengthening the technical and professional base, people's participation, association of organisations of the rural poor, staff participation and involvement in government management and decision-making process have also been emphasised time and again. The need for trained, content, motivated and competent personnel with high morale and positive work and social attitudes to help implement development programmes has also been similarly emphasised.

As discussed before, officials' perceptual analysis revealed a split between desired reforms and actual practice, a wide gap between 'saying' and 'doing'. This was also not unexpected as such a split is the hallmark of the present political and state ethos in the country. Such a culture is generally not conducive to development plans and projects. The officials' assessment of development performance corroborated it. They first recalled a variety of goals of development in India. These could be summarised as follows:

1. Citizen's economic betterment including providing them food, clothing, housing, education, etc.
2. Maintenance of price stability and controlling inflation in order to prevent industrial sickness.
3. Increasing productivity.
4. Poverty alleviation, social justice and equity to liberate them from socio-economic bondage.
5. Developing basic infrastructure, including land, for faster growth.

On further probing some of them remarked that development goals have been changing from plan to plan. At one time, community development sought to create infrastructural facilities like tube-wells. However, it was later found that the programme further enriched the rich and left the poor high and dry. By the time of the Sixth Plan, the emphasis had changed to direct poverty alleviation in order to improve the quality of life for the poor. Some of the senior officials were quite sceptical and one of them remarked, 'nobody knows what the development goals are. There are Planning Commission documents but you cannot make anything from them.' However, despite scepticism and differing perceptions, it was noteworthy that poverty alleviation and socio-economic development of the poor were very much in their perception.

Achievement of Development Goals

How far have the goals of development been achieved? The respondents gave their assessment, particularly of poverty allevia-tion goals. The overwhelming assessment, as seen in Table 3.6, was that such goals have not been achieved adequately. Further, as many as 80 per cent of them perceived that field information about development performance was seldom or never used for correction and/or improvement of programmes. There was hardly any learning from experience. In its absence, programmes were implemented only in a routine way, indicative of low concern for development performance.

Table 3.6
Development Related Achievements,
Information and Learning
(N = 21)

Items	Response (in per cent)	
How far have goals of develop-ment been achieved (goals such as self-reliance and alleviation of poverty)	*Yes, to some extent*	*No, not achieved*
	29	71
Extent to which information about development performance is used for further improvement	*Sometimes; often*	*Not at all; Rarely*
	20	80

How can Development Goals be Achieved?

The officials also suggested ways of improving developmental performance. These can be summarised as follows: (a) promoting village and household industries more vigorously with adequate marketing facilities; (b) power generation and supply of adequate electric power to industry and agriculture; (c) education for creating awareness and preparing the people for developmental efforts; (d) right selection of target groups for specific programmes and providing proper training to such people; (e) preparing field officials for implementing development plans and providing them with sufficient authority for initiating and executing such programmes; (f) political firmness for reducing people's dependence on the government, withdrawing subsidies after some time; (g) shifting priorities in favour of rural people to provide them with drinking water, electricity, education, health and other such facilities, proper and equitable distribution of material and non-material benefits; (h) developing infrastructure and income generating assistance on a continuing basis in order to provide employment; (i) increasing access to land for the poor through 'real' land reforms; (j) providing emphasis on quality as against the present emphasis on quantity and numbers in our development programmes.

The following suggestions regarding the need for specific actions emerged on further investigation and are as follows: (a) motivating community action and releasing people's initiative with involvement of public leaders and voluntary agencies; (b) developing individual initiative and entrepreneurship among the people; (c) stimulating sufficient economic growth for it to trickle down to the people and that there was no particular need for a direct programme of poverty alleviation; (d) continuous monitoring of development efforts and corrective action in the process; (e) creating infrastructure like marketing, transport, education and health facilities; (f) instead of subsidies, help should be provided in mobilising and organising the poor. 'It is a myth to say that the people have become dependent on the government. What is the government doing for them in any way? Not much.'

Divergence in Thinking

It was an interesting sample of thinking at the top bureaucratic level. Their thoughts raced from releasing market forces by demand and entrepreneurship, growth and trickle down theory on the one hand, to promotion of awareness among the rural poor and mobilising, educating and organising them for active involvement and assertion in developmental efforts on the other. Divergence of thinking suggested that senior bureaucrats did not constitute a monolithic system. The situation appeared like a cafetaria where you pick up things of your choice. Their thinking might indicate a concern for achieving better results but it also raised a question regarding the direction of development.

An assortment of viewpoints about the goals of development and policies for achieving development results matched well with the prevailing lack of harmony and coordination. While variety in thinking might promote creativity, too much divergence at the top could confuse and blunt the instrument (i.e., public administration) for implementing and achieving national goals. It also reflected political thinking inherent in our 'mixed' economy resulting in divergent, sometimes contradictory, policies. The social base of the bureaucracy, particularly the higher levels, is elite-oriented and their 'choices' are shaped by their background. No wonder poverty alleviation, equity and social justice programmes lack political and bureaucratic will. Not only are the stated goals not achieved under such conditions, but the 'rich' and 'resourceful' classes manage to corner the benefits, get richer and more powerful thus leaving the poor to nurture their poverty.

Forces Inhibiting and Facilitating Poverty
Alleviation and other Development Programmes

Senior officials also briefly analysed environmental forces constraining developmental performance. They also enumerated forces which could facilitate development. These forces are summarised in Table 3.7. Interestingly, they believed that a centralised administrative system was the most important impediment to development. They thought that the present system breeds apathy in seniors for their subordinates, weakens team work and harmonious implementation of programmes and creates similar problems which retard the progress of development.

Similarly, lack of a proper reward policy and accountability inhibited an effective implementation of programmes. The next important inhibiting force was the prevailing political culture characterised by undue political interference and lack of will for poverty alleviation. Thus, over two-thirds of their thoughts were

Table 3.7
Force Field Analysis of Development

Forces Inhibiting/ Constraining Development	Per cent of total Response	Forces Facilitating Development	Per cent of total Response
Centralisation; lack of superiors' support; secretariat apathy; lack of team work/sychronisation	31	Increasing awareness and assertion among the people	42
Politicisation and political interference; lack of political will for the poor	27	Increasing awareness of development and community needs in civil servants	42
Lack of a system of reward, punishment and accountability	15	Political support	08
Low motivation and commitment and negative attitudes of civil servants	15	Well organised administrative machinery	08
Lack of consciousness among the people; social forces like caste	12		

concerned with the inhibiting and negative forces emanating from the present administrative-cum-political system which pulled back programme implementation and retarded the fulfilment of development goals like poverty alleviation and social equity. They also perceived low motivation, low commitment to development and the negative attitude of civil servants on one hand and weak consciousness of the people and the presence of social forces like the caste system on the other as other important constraining forces. It is worth noting that structural constraints were uppermost in the minds of senior bureaucrats, who were themselves at the apex of this structure and who otherwise tended to behave in the direction of sustaining this system.

Facilitating Forces
Along with low commitment and motivation among civil servants and the presence of social forces like caste etc., senior officials also

perceived increasing awareness in them for community needs and development combined with increasing assertion among people themselves as the most important force pushing development programmes. They also saw some facilitating role in the political system as well as in the well organised administrative machinery. Therefore, there was a dialectic mirrored in their consciousness between rising awareness, assertion, consciousness of people including a section of civil servants on the one hand, and powerful constraints emanating from the dominant politico-social and administrative system on the other.

It is only the increasing awareness and assertion of the people which could overcome blocks created by an entrenched system and pave the way for successful efforts at poverty alleviation and nation-building. Inherent in this thinking is the challenge to generate a creative tension between forces which provide stability and those which drive change. The role of the leadership is to disturb the balance of forces in favour of change by facilitating awareness, organisation and assertion of the people in order to sow the seeds of change.

Monitoring and Learning

Formulation and implementation of developmental policies and programmes is a dynamic process. Receiving and utilising feedback in the development related learning process can, therefore, hardly be over-emphasised. Systematic data and appropriate efforts have a bearing on quality, self-reliance, participation, employment and the attainment of basic needs. Such efforts then percolate down to the people facilitating rural development (UNDP, 1979). Monitoring, therefore, means keeping track of the process of implementation which is expected to take place along with a particular predetermined trajectory. It is concerned with beneficiaries of the project, with the entire significance of stated goals, and with the obtained output rater than merely the final outcome. Over-emphasising the final outcome regardless of the process and the desired quality is like increasing speed irrespective of the direction (Hondle & Marcus, 1976). Therefore, monitoring is greatly emphasised in any planning process. From time to time the need for a continuous flow of correct and adequate information about ongoing projects and the related process in order to monitor progress towards the stated and predetermined goals has been repeatedly stressed in our plans. Monitoring, however, has not been satisfactory as has been noted from time to time by various reviews of different programmes.

Most senior bureaucrats—19 out of 21—expressed their clear dissatisfaction with the collection of information and monitoring of development programmes. They were dissatisfied with the usual 'returns filed' by various concerned functionaries by way of information about development programmes. The quality of such information was inevitably poor. There was no system for proper data collection and correct information. This task was generally left to the lowest functionaries like village level workers who were not competent to carry out this task.

Some of them held senior officials responsible for quantitative lapses and poor quality information as they insisted on physical and financial targets. The lower level beneficiaries only responded to pro formas sent by higher level departments and filed the returns as desired. This made the entire exercise routine and ritual. The government, therefore, gets the information they want. Furthermore, the field staff is usually overburdened with many other things and have neither the time nor the inclination to collect and file correct information. Thus, these bureaucrats believed that monitoring was the weakest link in development programmes. Some of them felt this rather strongly and believed that there was 'nothing like monitoring in the Government of India' and believed that decentralisation was the key to promoting adequate monitoring and learning processes. Rigid centralisation promoted and reinforced the 'pro forma' culture in the entire organisation. As mentioned above, the top management in the government considered the administrative and bureaucratic system itself responsible for lowering the quality of development programmes. Functionaries at the middle and field levels decode the message from the top leadership and pay attention to 'targets' rather than achieving quality in developmental performance in terms of socially important goals of poverty alleviation, equity, etc. Such a situation distorts the implementation process and facilitates its diversion in favour of the entrenched vested interests.

Administrative Structure and Behaviour: The Emerging Profile

The sample of respondents was too small to warrant firm inferences. However, the obtained sample of thoughts was rich, varied and suggestive of some meaningful lessons. The responses depicted some important dimensions of the existing administrative structure as well as behaviour. They also indicated some broad changes needed to reform the system of administration as well as obstacles which inhibit implementation of reforms.

Gap between Policy and Practices

The responses highlight the gap between policy and practice. The case of people's participation illustrates this point very well. The government has been repeatedly emphasising the need for people's participation in various development activities. The need for promoting and associating organisations of the rural poor has been further emphasised in this connection. However, this policy has hardly been practised. The same applies to the need for staff involvement and participation in government decision-making and the policy of land reforms. The existing system was perceived as highly centralised, rigidly rule-bound, unco-ordinated in its functioning, marked by lack of adequate expertise and preparedness for development and by poor working conditions for middle and lower level field employees.

The senior officials also perceived low morale among officials and employees, low concern for development in the bureaucracy and low probability of success in making the government work faster. They also thought that development performance was unsatisfactory and marked by the lack of proper monitoring and willingness to learn from experience.

Attitudinal Alignment with the Powerful Affluent

There was some awareness and concern among a small section of senior officials for a radical restructuring of the administrative system in order to make it more democratic and people oriented. They thought that the centralised and authoritarian system was responsible for negative attitudes and low morale and motivation among the personnel. However, the dominant view was in favour of maintaining the present system as the officials apprehended political interference and rise of trade unionism in the case of people's participation in development programmes and staff participation in decision-making. There was clear hostility towards political functionaries and trade unions. They saw a threat to law and order from organisations of the rural poor. Attitudinally, senior bureaucrats seemed to be clearly aligned with the affluent and powerful sections of society, particularly in rural areas.

Subjective Contradictions

There were contradictions—sometimes a split—in their thoughts, particularly when it came to implementing reforms. While showing themselves to be liberal and democratic, they would hold the centralised authoritarian system responsible for poor performance. Such liberal ideas also went into policy-making. While confronted with the implementation of some such ideas, they would see many 'threats'—political interference, trade unionism, indiscipline, their neutrality etc. Such contradictions are resolved by not implementing policies, i.e., by perpetuating the same system which they decry as non-performing and demoralising. Such attitudes reflect their alignment with the existing political and social forces which stood to gain by centralised and non-participatory regulatory administration.

The bureaucratic ambivalence also came out in their analysis of forces which could facilitate the desired changes. They perceived the democratic force as the most important one for pushing the administration towards greater social accountability and responsiveness. However, they were not willing to contribute to the release of such forces. In fact, if anything, they would side with the opposite forces.

Split between Word and Deed

An analysis of dominant thoughts at the apex of the Indian bureaucracy, therefore, revealed some sort of split between the 'desirable' and what actually happened in practice—a split between word and deed. This split was one of the reasons for the poor functioning of administration as a whole in terms of lowering their efficacy, credibility and responsiveness and by isolating them from the people. Such an administrative situation and bureaucratic personality were indeed not likely to promote fulfilment of the stated developmental goals, i.e., poverty alleviation, social justice and social development. Such a situation cannot remain confined only to the apex level—the senior management of the government. It was likely to percolate down to all levels of the bureaucracy with concomitant implications for development programmes.

4

Middle Managers in Government

The senior officials' perceptions, as discussed in chapter 3, were utilised in designing a study for intermediate and lower level officials constituting the middle management in government. The top managements' perceptions suggested some dimensions for the proposed study of work-behaviour, social behaviour and development behaviour at middle (and lower) levels of our bureaucracy. The main purpose of the proposed study of middle managers was to explore their perceptions pertaining to work, social issues and development.

INSTRUMENTS FOR THE STUDY

It was decided to use two ready instruments, namely, work questionnaire (WQ) and general opinion questionnaire (GOQ) for obtaining perceptions regarding the work situation and attitudinal data indicative of their social outlook. These instruments have been developed and used for similar studies of managers and employees in public and private sector enterprises and elsewhere. These measures have consistently shown high reliability and validity (Mehta, 1976; Rao and Mehta, 1978; Rao and Mehta, 1979; and Mehta and Jain, 1979).

The Work Questionnaire

The WQ provides data about the quality of work-life as perceived by the respondents. Data are obtained with regard to four dimensions—perceived influence in work-life, perceived amenities at workplace/work-life, perceived nature of job, and perceived supervisory behaviour/practice. The questionnaire consists of 24 items, six each for four dimensions of perceived quality of work-life. Such data also indicate the perceived organisational and work climate obtaining in a given organisation (Mehta, 1976) and employees' satisfaction at work (Mehta, 1977a).

Six items composing the scale for perceived influence in work-life provide data regarding practices, such as, information sharing, availability of influence in decision-making regarding employees' welfare, grievance redressal, influence in decision-making regarding nature and schedule of work, inter-personal listening and working together, and freedom of speech and opinion at the workplace. Work amenities included benefits like education for children, medical facilities for families etc., perception regarding salary, drinking water, canteen and catering, recreation, and housing made available by the organisation. The nature of job included opportunity for learning new things, variety in jobs, challenge in jobs, freedom and autonomy, significance and meaningfulness of jobs perceived to be available in the organisation. Supervisory behaviour/practice consists of the relationship between superiors and subordinates, respect for suggestions made by employees, appreciation of good work, superiors' image of subordinates' capability, planning done by superiors, and superiors' support to subordinates perceived to be available at the workplace. The questionnaire is presented in Appendix II.

Socio-Political Outlook: The GOQ

The GOQ was used to obtain data on their socio-political outlook. The GOQ provides data on personality orientations relating to socio-political matters under four dimensions. Misanthropy–Faith in People consists of eight items seeking response to classes such as rich and poor in society, family planning, bad persons working with good persons, resolution of social evils and personal conflicts, mutual trust, nationalisation of industry, different religious groups working together, and meaningfulness of elections. The sense of political powerlessness–efficacy (SPP–SPE) consists of four items concerning understanding the functioning of government, importance of voting, influencing events in politics and influencing public affairs. Sense of political normlessness–accepting regime norms (SPN) consists of three items on prevailing political culture, namely, functioning of political parties, influence of vested interests in government and people's participation in government. The fourth scale on social dogmatism versus liberalism consists of four items concerning the acceptance of supreme power, compulsory military training, moral character and faith in religion and God. The questionnaire is given in Appendix III.

The Development Questionnaire (DEQ)

It was decided to develop a new questionnaire for obtaining data on development related behavioural orientations. This was designed on the basis of perceptual data obtained from senior officials as discussed in chapter 3 and in earlier studies (Mehta, 1985; Mehta, 1985 a, and Faculty of Management Studies, 1985).

Several relevant items were written for inclusion in this questionnaire. These were discussed internally. Finally, 18 items were selected and formulated. These items pertain to people's participation and organisation of rural workers; information and use of development programmes; concern and preparedness for development programmes; employees' involvement in administration; evaluation of development performance; staff associations and staff participation; knowledge about environmental forces; red-tapism and flexibility; and job satisfaction. The content of items is set out in Table 5.1 and the questionnaire in Appendix I. Details regarding development and validation of the instrument are discussed in chapter 6.

Middle Level Civil Servants

It was decided to study a group of middle to intermediate level officials working in states at secretariat/headquarters, districts and lower levels as well as some working at the central level. The idea was to get a cross-section of officials representing a variety of development and regulatory functions and posted at various levels. The need was also there to get a quick sample to enable proper data collection. With this in view, training calendars of several institutes of public administration were examined to locate such development related training programme which could provide the necessary sample. The institutes at Nainital (U.P.), Jaipur (Rajasthan), Chandigarh (Haryana) and Mysore (Karnataka) agreed to collaborate in data collection. Appropriate training events were then selected in order to obtain an adequate sample of the desired categories of officials. This procedure enabled quick data collection from relevant personnel at one place. However, data collection was in no way connected with the training programme itself. The groups thus selected belonged to state cadres and some to central services. The instruments were administered to them with full awareness that they were collaborating in a research programme and not providing data as inputs in respective training courses. All questionnaires were administered under personal supervision of the research project personnel. Thus, a group of 169 officials checked the questionnaires during June–August, 1985.

Departmental/Functional Background of the Respondents
The respondents eventually selected for data collection came from a variety of development related departments and also from those performing administrative and regulatory functions. Thus, a large number of them were working in departments/agencies engaged in promoting and maintaining agriculture, animal husbandry, cooperatives, irrigation, afforestation, water supply, industrial safety, research and experimentation, energy, labour and employment, land development, food and suplies etc. Some respondents were working in departmental headquarters, state secretariat and central offices in administrative capacities. While those who came from departments like police, taxation, prison, defence and railway administration etc., were also scattered in their postings at state, district, block and tehshil levels, some of them were located in central departments. It was this variety of development experience which differentiated various small groups within the total group of respondents involved in providing the necessary data for the study. Such richness of background and experience served the purpose of the study, particularly regarding work and development related orientations.

Personal and Organisational Background
Analyses of the organisation and personal data indicated that, 43 per cent of them came from the age-group of 46–55 years and another 35 per cent from the 41–45 years ago-group. Thus, 78 per cent of the sample came from the age group of 41–55 years with the median age at about 45 years. They had put in long years of service, some 38 per cent of them between 16 and 25 years and another 23 per cent more than 25 years of service. As regards

education, some 42 per cent were graduates, 52 per cent post-graduates and the remaining were matriculates. Additionally, some 44 per cent reported some technical and professional quali-fications. They came from different departments and postings—some positioned very close to and with direct involvement in implementing development programmes and some placed remotely to them, with no direct involvement in any specific development programme.

The officials' age and length of service in government, as could be expected, were highly inter-correlated. Higher the age, greater was the income and length of service as well as greater stagnation as indicated by the number of years spent in the same position/job without promotion to the next higher position. Interestingly, the educational level revealed a negative correlation ($r = -.23$, $P<.01$) with age indicating that younger officials (in the sample) were more educated than their older (not necessarily senior) colleagues. Another significant feature was that technically trained/educated officials showed greater stagnation ($r = .28$, $P<.01$) than others. They also showed higher income. It was also noteworthy that posting, i.e., position proximity to development (PPD) as explained above and discussed later (in chapter 9), revealed no correlation with any of the remaining six variables, suggesting that it was an important organisational variable by itself.

Work-Related Perceptions and Sample Background

Position proximity to development showed highly significant negative correlation with perceived work amenities. It was negative with regard to the nature of supervisory behaviour/practice. There-fore, the preliminary analyses suggested that officials posted in departments which were directly involved in implementing develop-mental programmes, such as offices at district and block levels, were clearly dissatisfied with amenities available to them at their workplace. They clearly felt alienated from their working environ-ment. Interestingly, supervisory behaviour/practices also formed part of this working environment and they were not happy with them either. This was the most conspicuous and significant finding indicative of a deep sense of resentment among the concerned officials. Another important source of dissatisfaction was a lack of promotional avenues in their work-life. Greater the period of stagnation, lower was the satisfaction with influence and work amenities (although statistically not significant). Interestingly, the sense of resentment and unhappiness came not so much from the nature of job performed over a long period of time or from seniors. Rather, it seemed to arise from the denial of influence and amenities which come with higher positions in the organisation. Another interesting finding was the relationship between income and satisfaction with amenities. It seemed that higher the income, greater was the satisfaction with increasing amenities at the workplace. Salary itself was one important component of work amenities and those placed in higher income groups felt satisfied with their working environment.

An increasing sense of dissatisfaction with the available influence at the place of work and with the working environment among officials located closer to development implementation was an important finding for purposes of the present study. Implications of such dissatisfaction could be many for the quality of programme implementation on the ground. We will revert to this issue in later chapters when some more data would be presented and discussed. Another seemingly important finding with implications for programme implementation was the increasing sense of satisfaction with the nature of their job among officials with higher/increasing education. Interestingly, officials with technical training did not show any differentiated feelings with any of the four dimensions of the perceived work situation.

Socio-Political Tendencies and Background
As mentioned before, younger officials were more educated and the higher the official's age, the greater was the length of service. Younger officials were also socially more liberal. Significantly, the older ones were socially more conservative and dogmatic ($r = .27$, $P<.01$). The same was true of the length of service. Taking this as the criterion, the (age and length of service) 'senior' middle level officials in the government were socially more dogmatic ($r = .23$, $P<.01$) than their 'juniors'. Education appeared to be a liberalising force. The more the education, the lower was the conservative–dogmatic tendency ($r = -.26$, $P<.01$). Significantly, both education and income tended to reduce the sense of political powerlessness. The higher the education ($r = .19$, $P<.05$) and income ($r = .18$, $P<.05$), the lower was the sense of political powerlessness (or

higher the sense of political efficacy). These findings were similar to findings regarding the sense of political efficacy reported elsewhere (Mehta, 1975; 1976a; 1977 by 1981).

There was, however, no significant relationship of the background variables with the sense of misanthropy (i.e., lack of faith in people). Officials posted very close to and with direct involvement in development programmes, i.e., those at the cutting edge, tended to show significantly greater acceptance of political (regime) norms, suggesting their somewhat greater integration ($r = -.16$, P <.05) with the ruling political culture. Taken together, highly educated and technically trained middle managers posted closer to development implementation tended to show greater closeness to and integration with the prevailing norms of the regime and the political culture.

Thus, middle managers participating in this study came from various departments, postings and states with different educational backgrounds, some with technical professional education. They were spread over different age-groups with varying length of service along with varying work related perceptions and political orientations: some closely aligned with the ruling political culture and working environment while others modestly to strongly alienated from them. The variety in the background to the respondents was likely to provide a corresponding variety in their responses (and behaviour) thus yielding a representative cross-section of development related bureaucratic orientations, work related attitudes, and social outlook. The group of middle and intermediate level officials obtained for the study seemed appropriate for a further detailed investigation regarding development and bureaucratic behaviour.

5

Development Related Bureaucratic Behaviour: Construct Analysis and Validation

The development questionnaire (DEQ) consists of 18 items, as mentioned in chapter 4 and seen in Appendix I. A brief variable description along with variables' numbers (to be used in further analyses and discussion) and abbreviated terms are given in Table 5.1 for ready reference. The four dimensions of perceived quality of work-life (as discussed in chapter 4) namely, influence, amenities, nature of job, and supervisory behaviour, showed varying relationships with responses on DEQ. For instance, assessment of existing level of people's participation (V–18), assessment of employee involvement in administration (V–22), officers' job satisfaction (V–24) and programme feedback (V–31) revealed significant positive correlations with the perceived influence at work, job satisfaction and satisfaction with supervisory behaviour. There were some items which showed a relationship only with the nature of job. These were employee job satisfaction (V–25) and importance of continuing information for improving programmes (V–29). Some items like staff-preparedness (V–20) and superior's role in developing staff preparedness (V–21) did not show any relationship with the various dimensions of perceived work-life. In all, 12 of the 18 items revealed a significant relationship with the perceived supervisory behaviour, eight with the perceived nature of job, and six with the perceived influence at work. Perceived work amenities showed significant correlations with only two items, namely, importance of people's participation (V–17) and assessment of self-reliance and internal capability (V–16).

It was clear that development related (DEQ) items, selected on the basis of earlier studies and the perceptions of senior managers,

Table 5.1
Development Related Bureaucratic Orientations:
Variable Descriptions

Bureaucratic Behaviour	Description
V–16 (ICA)	Assessment of Achievement of Self-reliance and Internal Capability
V–17 (PPI)	Importance of People's Participation in Development
V–18 (PPA)	Assessment of Existing Level of People's Participation
V–19 (ORW)	Importance of Organisation of Rural Workers in Development
V–20 (SPE)	Staff Preparedness and Expertise for Expanding Public Administration
V–21 (SRD)	Superiors' Role in Developing Staff Preparedness
V–22 (EIA)	Assessment of Employees Involvement in Public Administration
V–23 (GDC)	Need to Generate Development Concern among Employees
V–24 (OJS)	Officers Job Satisfaction
V–25 (EJS)	Employees Job Satisfaction
V–26 (SPM)	Staff Participation in Management of Government Departments
V–27 (PSP)	Promotion of Staff Participation by Staff Associations and Employees Unions
V–28 (EFP)	Extent to which Environmental Factors taken into Account in Programmes
V–29 (IFP)	Importance of Information on Continuing Basis for Improvement of Ongoing Programmes
V–30 (PIC)	Extent to which Programme Information is Collected
V–31 (PFU)	Extent to which Programme Feedback and Information Used
V–32 (CDP)	Extent to which Conflicts in Development Programmes Occur
V–33 (SRT)	Probability of Success in Reducing Red-tapism

showed variations when compared with the perceived quality of work-life. Such item-variability suggested the possibility of tapping variations in respondents' development behaviour.

Inter-Correlations

The inter-correlations among DEQ items, confirmed the view that they tended to reveal different behavioural tendencies. For instance, assessment of internal capability (V–16) showed significant correlations only with two items—supervisors' role (V–21) and programme feedback (V–31). Similarly, importance of people's participation (V–17) showed significant correlation with only three items—superiors' role (V–21), development concern (V–23) and continuing information (V–29). Some clusters seem to emerge among variables 19 to 25 and variables 28 to 31. However, such clusters in various DEQ items indicating different bureaucratic orientations to development became clear only after the obtained data were factor-analysed.

Varimax Rotated Principal Factors

All the 33 variables, consisting of seven background variables, four measures of perceived quality of work-life, four measures of socio-political outlook (personality) and 18 development related responses (on DEQ) were processed for principal factors and rotated by the varimax method. The extraction of factors was stopped when the obtained eigen value dropped below 1. Thus, 12 factors were extracted, each having an eigen value of more than 1.

These factors together accounted for 68 per cent of the variance in the combination of measures processed in the matrix. However, we would not describe the various factors in the order of their extraction. One of the main objectives of the present study was to identify important development related bureaucratic orientations among middle level officials in the government. We would first explain the *constructs* used to describe various development related bureaucratic orientations as extracted and then take up other factors in the next chapter. The full factor matrix is presented in Appendix IV.

Participation Orientation (NV–3)

The need to generate concern for development among the employees (variable 23 on DEQ) showed a high loading on Factor 3 as seen in Table 5.2. The importance of people's participation and the probability of success in efforts for reducing red-tapism also showed significant loadings on this factor (these, however, showed higher loadings on other factors and are, therefore, included there as discussed below). This suggested that the factor indicated an orientation supportive of development, and flexibility and forward

looking attitude in day-to-day administration. It was associated
with a socially liberal attitude, as shown by the negative loading of
conservative–dogmatism (V–11) and positive loading of education
on this factor. This factor, therefore, indicated a liberal, forward
looking and participatory orientation.

Table 5.2
New Variables (Scales) Derived from Factor Analysis:
Factors 3 & 4: Participation Orientation
(NV–3)

Variable	Loadings		h^2
	Factor 3	Factor 4	
19 Importance of ORW in development		.81	.73
23 Need to generate development concern among employees	.61		.58
26 Desirability of staff participation in administration within government		.71	.66
Other Measures With Significant Loadings on this Factor			
17 Importance of people's participation in development	.44	.29	.70
33 Probability of success in reducing red-tapism	.36		.56
24 Officers's job satisfaction		.40	.68
11 Conservative–dogmatism	−.46		.55
3 Education	.68		.55
7 Income	.40		.74
2 Age	−.23		.81
6 Stagnation	−.24		.57
18 Assessment of people's participation		.24	

   Importance of the organisation of rural workers in development
and desirability of staff participation in administration (management) within the government showed high loadings on Factor 4, as
can be seen from Table 5.2. Importance of people's participation
also revealed a significant loading on this factor. This factor,
therefore, seemed to suggest a similar liberal participatory orientation. Principal factors are supposed to be independent of each
other. However, here they revealed significant inter-correlations,
as discussed later. Therefore, independence of factors may not be

empirical, but may be imposed by the model (Rummel, 1968; Harman, 1967). A combination of Factors 3 and 4 appeared more realistic. These three items, showing highest loadings on these two factors, were, therefore, put together to form a single measure for the present study. It was designated as participation orientation (in development related bureaucratic behaviour). It later showed good reliability and validity, as can be seen from Table 5.9. Interestingly, this was associated more with younger, flexible, upwardly mobile, liberal and forward looking officials.

Performance Justification (NV–4)

Positive evaluation of the extent to which development information was presently collected (V–30) and the extent to which such information was utilised for improving programmes (V–31) revealed high loadings on Factors (see Table 5.3). An interesting

Table 5.3
New Variables (Scales) Derived from Factor Analysis:
Factor 5: Performance Justification
(NV–4)

Variable	Loading on Factor 5	h^2
30 Extent to which development information is presently collected	.54	.58
31 Extent to which such collected information is utilised for improving programmes	.60	.67
Other Measures with Significant Loadings on this Factor		
1 Position proximity to development Work	.62	.59
10 Sense of political normlessness	−.37	.64
13 Perceived amenities at work	−.60	.71
19 Importance of rural workers' organisations	.29	.73
25 Employee job satisfaction	.33	.70

aspect of this factor was the high positive loading of officer's placement and its proximity to development work. Greater the proximity to development work on the ground, higher was the orientation indicated by this factor. Uniformly favourable assessment of certain important functions of development personnel, particularly among officials positioned closer to field and implementation suggested this to be a behavioural orientation to justify performance in ongoing programmes and practices. It is significant to note that the tendency exhibited here was in sharp contrast to the perception of senior officials as presented in Table 3.6, where nearly 80 per cent felt that development information was rarely used for further improving the programme. It seemed to suggest that officials high on this orientation tended to justify their own performance. The construct here was designated as an orientation for performance justification.

It was interesting to note (see Table 5.3) that the higher this orientation, greater was the sense of dissatisfaction with existing amenities at work (see Appendix I for items) alongwith a greater sense of stagnation in one's career in the government. Another significant feature of this orientation was its association with greater acceptance and/or conformism with the prevailing political system and regime norms (opposite of the sense of political norm-lessness; see Appendix III for items). We will come back to this aspect later in the discussion.

Complacency (NV–6)

This factor (Factor 7) was mainly informed by a very high loading of staff preparedness for expanding public administration (V–20) (see Table 5.4). Employee involvement in administration (V–22) revealed a high loading on Factor 10 and a significant loading on Factor 7. These factors seemed to indicate a similar tendency, i.e., to assess staff competence and involvement favourably. It may be recalled here that senior officials (see Table 3.3) were not sure of the competence and preparedness of employees and about their concern for development. Therefore, this tendency suggested a sense of complacency and was designated as such. This was further confirmed by favourable assessment of existing people's participation (see Table 3.1 for senior officials assessment) and a strong denial of conflicts in various development programmes (V–32) as indicated by a high negative loading on Factor 7. This orientation of complacency was also somewhat correlated with positive assessment of achievement of internal capability (V–16) and probability of success in reducing red-tapism (V–33). These three items (variables 18, 20, 22 on DEQ) were, therefore, combined to form a measure of bureaucratic complacency (opposite of vigilance). It should be noted here that performance justification and complacency emerged as two different constructs indicating these to be two different orientations.

Table 5.4
New Variables (Scales) Derived from Factor Analysis
Factors 7 & 10: Complacency
(NV–6)

| Variable | Loadings | | h^2 |
	Factor 7	Factor 10	
18 Evaluation of existing people's participation	.41	—	.67
20 Evaluation of staff preparedness for expanding public administration	.82	—	.75
22 Evaluation of employee involvement in administration	.21	.62	.71
Other Measures with Significant Loadings on this Factor			
32 Conflicts in various development programmes	−.75		.62
25 Employee job satisfaction	.45		.70
28 Extent to use environmental factors in development programmes	−.32		.68
10 Sense of political normlessness		.34	.64
11 Dogmatic–conservatism		−.25	.55
16 Assessment of self-reliance and internal capability in the rural poor	.20		.67
33 Probability of success in reducing red-tapism	.23		.56

Coaching–Dependence Orientation (NV–7)

Assessment of 'seniors' role in developing staff preparedness and expertise for expanding jobs (V–21) revealed a very high loading on Factor 8, as can be seen from Table 5.5. Interestingly, job satisfaction (V–24, see Appendix I) showed significant negative loading and the need to generate development concern in employees (V–23) revealed a positive loading on this factor. Furthermore, it seemed to be associated with a favourable attitude towards staff associations (V–26). This factor, therefore, indicated some kind of expectation from the seniors in those not so much satisfied with their jobs and at the same time realising (or being aware) that they needed to have concern for development work. It seemed to indicate an orientation of expecting coaching, (maybe help as defined by the respondents) from the superiors.

Table 5.5
New Variables (Scales) Derived from Factor Analysis:
Factor 8: Coaching–Dependence Orientation
(NV–7)

Variable	Loading on Factor 8	h^2
16 Evaluation of self-reliance and internal capability development in rural poor	.30	.67
21 Senior's role in developing staff preparedness	.82	.75
Other Measures with Significant Loadings on this Factor		
11 Conservative–dogmatism	.38	.55
23 Need to generate development concern	.30	.58
25 Employee job satisfaction	−.23	.70
24 Officers job satisfaction	−.34	.68
26 Role of staff associations in promoting staff participation	.25	.66
1 Position proximity to development	−.25	.59
6 Years on the same position	.29	.57
17 Importance of peoples' participation	.25	.70

It is interesting to note that the greater this orientation, the greater was the conservative–dogmatic outlook (see Table 5.5). It suggested that expectations of subordinates from superiors were associated with a conservative social outlook which informed the relationship between the two in this role-set. It seemed to indicate a tendency for coaching (tutoring) as well as dependence. It was noteworthy that this orientation was more among officials placed some distance from development work and may be among those suffering from stagnation in their career. This was designated as the coaching–dependence orientation. This carried some help giving– help seeking tendency informed specifically by a hierarchical bureaucratic relationship.

'Association' Orientation

A favourable attitude to staff associations and their role in promoting staff participation in management in government (V–27) showed a high loading on Factor 11, as can be seen from Table 5.6. Persons

Table 5.6
New Variables (Scales) Derived from Factor Analysis:
'Association' Orientation
(NV–9)

Variables	Loading on Factor 11	h^2
27 Evaluation of the role of staff associations in promoting staff participation in management in government	.65	.68
28 Evaluation of use of environmental (limiting and facilitating) factors taken into account in initiating and executing programmes	.63	.69
33 Evaluation of chances of success in efforts for minimising red-tapism	.56	.56
Others Measures with Significant Loadings on this Factor		
1 Position proximity to development	−.28	.59
30 Extent to which programme information is collected	.28	.58
31 Extent to which programme information is used for improving programmes	.34	.67

with such an orientation had positively assessed the use of environmental factors (V–28) in executing programmes and positive probability of success in efforts for minimising red-tapism (V–33). This indicated a flexible attitude to the rule bound administrative structure. For want of better description, this was designated as 'association' orientation. Interestingly, it seemed to be somewhat greater among officials who were remote to development work (i.e., secretariat officials and employees). It seemed to imply some collective action orientation but not necessarily with a liberal social attitude. Performance justification items also revealed positive loadings on this factor, suggesting that this orientation was not so much associated with the concern to improve performance.

Feedback Orientation

Importance of continuing field information for improving development programmes showed a very high loading on Factor 12 (see
Table 5.7). This, therefore, indicated a feedback orientation and

Table 5.7
New Variables (Scales) Derived from Factor Analysis:
Factor 12: Feedback Orientation
(NV–10)

Variable	Loading on Factor 12	h^2
17 Importance of people's participation in development programmes	.47	.70
29 Importance of continuing information about development programmes for improvement	.82	.69
Other Measures with Significant Loadings on this Factor		
6 Year on the same position	.31	.57
10 Sense of political normlessness	−.32	.64
9 Sense of political powerlessness	−.26	.66
14 Nature of job	.22	.64
28 Extent to which EF taken into account	.23	.68

was designated as such. Officials showing this orientation also
tended to perceive their jobs as rich and meaningful (for nature of
job see Appendix II). Interestingly, this orientation was associated
with a greater acceptance of regime norms and a greater sense of
political efficacy. These two dimensions of political behaviour
seemed to suggest that such respondents were active supporters of
the political system. The extent of their concern for performance
was not clear from this analysis. However, perceptions of a
meaningful job and feedback orientation did indicate some
performance orientation.

COMMON VARIANCE IN THE MATRIX

The DEQ, consisting of 15 items (for DEQ see Appendix I),
seemed to tap six different development related bureaucratic

orientations in behaviour. The remaining three items, namely, officers' job satisfaction (V–24), employees' job satisfaction (V–25) and conflicts in development programmes (V–32), were eliminated from the questionnaire. The first two served the same purpose as items composing nature of job (in WQ). These also did not show high loadings on any of the factors. The third item revealed a very high negative loading on complacency and was used to define this construct. Six orientations, thus defined and identified, accounted for some 38 per cent, in the common variance of 68 per cent in the factor matrix. Thus, participation orientation (NV–3) accounted for 13.7 per cent (combination of Factors 3 and 4); performance justification (NV–4) 5.7 per cent; complacency (NV–6) (combination of factors 1 and 10) 8.5 per cent; coaching–dependence (NV–7) 3.7 per cent; 'association' orientation (NV–9) 3.2 per cent, and feedback orientation (NV–10) 3.1 per cent variance in the matrix. It was interesting that about half of the common variance was accounted for by these six DRBO's and the remaining half was shared by four measures of perceived quality of work-life, four measures of socio-political outlook (personality) and seven organisational–personal background variables.

Measurement of Development Related Bureaucratic Orientations (DRBO)

Stability of Mean Scores

Constructs of the six development related bureaucratic orientations (DRBO) in behaviour, as discussed above, and their measures as formed by respective DEQ items were further processed for central tendencies and standard errors etc. The obtained results are presented in Table 5.8. The obtained mean scores for the six new variables, i.e., NV–3, NV–4, NV–6, NV–7, NV–9 and NV–10, appeared to be stable and trustworthy, at 95 per cent level of confidence. Low standard errors (SE) in each case suggested reasonable reliability of respective measures of these six variables.

Validity of the Measures

The communality values (h²) obtained in factor-analysis (see

Table 5.8
Officials' Development Related Bureaucratic Orientations (DRBO): Means and Standard Deviations

DRBO	N	Mean	S.D.	S.E.	Minimum Score	Maximum Score	95 per cent Conf.	Int. For Mean
Participation Orientation	150	10.15	1.54	0.13	5.00	12.00	9.91	10.40
Performance Justification	164	5.04	1.57	0.12	2.00	8.00	4.79	5.28
Complacency	164	9.34	1.95	0.15	5.00	14.00	9.04	9.64
Coaching–Dependence	150	5.74	0.96	0.08	3.00	8.00	5.58	5.89
'Association' Orientation	150	8.13	1.89	0.15	3.00	12.00	7.83	8.44
Feedback Orientation	150	7.76	0.82	0.67	4.00	13.00	7.63	7.89

Tables 5.2 to 5.7) for the respective variables (see Appendix I for items on DEQ) constituting the six orientations ranging between .56 (for V–33 in NV–9) to .75 (for V–20 in NV–6 and V–21 in NV–7). Since construct validity of a measure is equal to its communality (Kerlinger, 1978: 469–71), i.e., proportion of common variance to total variance, it tends to range between the obtained h^2 values of individual variables constituting measures of new variables. Thus, construct validity coefficients for measures of each construct or new variable obtained by averaging the respective h^2 values are seen in Table 5.9. Common variance in each construct was about two-thirds of the total variance. Theoretically, individual variables constituting various measures were highly correlated with the designated constructs indicating good validity in each case.

Table 5.9
*Construct Validity and Reliability
Coefficients of Measures of Development
Related Bureaucratic Orientations*
(N = 119)

	New Variables					
	NV–3	NV–4	NV–6	NV–7	NV–9	NV–10
Validity* Coefficient	.66	.62	.71	.71	.64	.69
Reliability† Coefficient	.65	.81	.88	.63	.57	.60

* derived from h^2 values
† derived from analysis of variance

Reliability of the New Variables
Reliability of a measure is always greater or equal to its communality (h^2) obtained in factor-analysis (Kerlinger, 1978: 665). As such, reliability of new variables should at least have been equal if not higher than their validity coefficients. As can be seen from Table 5.9, the test of reliability was higher (than validity) at .81 for performance justification and .88 for complacency. In all other cases, it was either almost equal or somewhat lower. For participation orientation, reliability was .65 (validity = .66); for

association orientation, .57 (validity = .64); and for feedback
orientation, reliability was .60 (validity = .69). It seemed that the
wording of the items (see Appendix I) and the mode of obtaining
responses etc., needed attention and necessary modifications in
further research.

DEVELOPMENT RELATED BUREAUCRATIC ORIENTATIONS: INTER-CORRELATIONS

Was there any inter-relationship and/or any other emerging cluster
in the new variables of development related bureaucratic orientations? Some orientations such as participation orientation and
feedback orientation on one hand, and performance justification
and complacency on the other, seemed to overlap. Results confirmed such a view. Participation orientation was significantly
correlated (r = .17, P<.01) with feedback orientation. Performance
justification was highly correlated with complacency (r = .44,
P<.005) and with 'association' orientation (r = .26, P<.005),
complacency showed correlations of .22 and .20 respectively with
coaching and association orientation (both P<.005). The latter
two were also inter-correlated significantly. The results seem to
show two distinct clusters, formed by 'participation' orientation
and feedback orientation on one hand, and by the remaining four
on the other. In addition to mutuality, feedback orientation shows
a significant correlation (r = .15 P<.05) with coaching (which may
contain help). In other words, officials with greater orientation for
feedback from development performance also showed greater
willingness to learn. The results seemed to suggest two broad and
almost distinct behavioural orientations, justification–complacency
on one hand and participation and feedback orientation on the
other. If it was so, then the latter characteristic probably indicated
a concern for pro-people development performance and the
former some kind of influence and status orientated behaviour.
We will come back to this point later while explaining variance
in these bureaucratic behavioural orientations in chapter 7, when
the meaning of these orientations would be further clarified.

6

Perceived Quality of Work-Life, Personality and Other Measures: Construct Development and Validation

The four measures of work related perceptions, namely, perceived quality of work-life, influence at work, amenities at work, nature of job and supervisory behaviour, as described in chapter 4 (for the items see Appendix II) clustered in the first principal factor as seen in Table 6.1. This factor was designated as perceived quality of work-life (PQWL). It accounted for 12.5 per cent component in the common variance of 68 per cent. This composite factor also indicated respondents' sense of satisfaction with certain important dimensions of the structure and functioning of government organ- isations. High loadings of perceived influence and perceived supervisory behaviour on this factor suggested that it was more a power and relationship oriented construct. As expected, satisfaction with amenities at work also showed its highest loading on PQWL. However, this loading was much lower than those shown by the other three PQWL dimensions including perceived nature of job. Thus, variance in this factor was contributed by both the work context/work environment as well as the perceived content of jobs. The composite measure, therefore, revealed an interactive assessment of the work environment, and climate and content of work. Here, the resultant response indicated overall satisfaction, as shaped by certain attributes of the organisation and as mirrored in the consciousness of the respondents (for a review of the literature on 'climate' and 'satisfaction' see Sharma, 1987). The dichotomy between content of work and context of work, often described as motivators and hygiene factors (Herzberg, 1966, 1968), was clearly rejected by the findings here. The results provided a striking confirmation of similar findings earlier (Mehta, 1977a; Mehta, 1978).

Table 6.1
New Variables (Scales) Derived from Factor Analysis: Factor 1:
Perceived Quality of Work-Life (Work Satisfaction)
(NV–1)

Variables	Loading on Factor 1	h^2
12 Perceived influence in work-life	.85	.77
13 Perceived amenities at/in workplace/work-life	.49	.71
14 Perceived nature of job	.74	.64
15 Perceived supervisory behaviour	.81	.78
Other Measures with Significant Loadings on this Factor		
23 Need to generate concern for development among the employees	.40	.58
24 Officer's job satisfaction	.44	.68
09 Sense of political powerlessness	−.30	.66
10 Sense of political normlessness	−.45	.64
16 Evaluation of self-reliance achieved among the rural poor	.28	.67
18 Assessment of existing people's participation	.35	.67
22 Assessment of EI in development	.40	.71
25 Employee job satisfaction	.27	.70
28 Extent to which EF taken into account	.23	.68
31 Extent to which programme feedback exists	.23	.67

Perceived Quality of Work-Life and Political Alienation

The results presented in Table 6.1 provided confirmation of another important hypothesis regarding work alienation and political alienation. Earlier findings (Mehta, 1976a; 1981) suggested a close relationship between middle managers' alienation at work and outside, particularly with regard to the political situation. Significant negative loadings of the sense of political powerlessness and sense of political normlessness on this factor clearly suggested that greater the work satisfaction, higher was the sense of political efficacy (opposite of powerlessness) and stronger was the integration and acceptance of regime norms of the prevailing political system (for measures see Appendix III). In other words, work alienated (as indicated by low work satisfaction—the opposite of satisfaction with PQWL) middle managers in the government also seemed to show higher political alienation as indicated by a greater sense of political powerlessness and political normlessness.

It was interesting to note that government officials with a greater sense of satisfaction and/or integration with their work as well as the political situation tended to assess gains of development more positively, as indicated by significant loadings of evaluation of self-reliance, existing people's participation and employee involvement in administration on this factor of PQWL. We shall come back to this hypothesis while explaining the variance in PQWL in chapter 8.

Means and Standard Errors in Perceived Quality of Work-Life

Table 6.2 reports mean scores, standard errors etc., as obtained for the four measures, namely, perceived influence, perceived amenities, nature of job and perceived supervisory behaviour as well as the new variables—the construct of work-satisfaction and PQWL. As is evident, the obtained SE in each single case was very low suggesting high reliability of these measures. The mean scores were stable at 95 per cent level of confidence. The results in Table 6.2 suggests high test-reliability in each case including that of the new measure of PQWL.

Construct Validity of Measures of PQWL

High communality (h^2) values for each of the four measures constituting the new variables of perceived quality of work-life (PQWL) indicated their high construct validity. Such coefficients are reproduced in Table 6.3 (along with test-reliability) for ready reference. It was clear that each measure of perceived work situation showed a high correlation with the theoretical construct constituting the new variable of work satisfaction/perceived quality of worklife. The composite measure (NV–1) of the construct PQWL (used in later analysis) itself showed high validity as indicated by an average $h^2 = .72$. It was indeed the most important and powerful variable, the first principal component factor in the matrix of 33 variables, accounting for 18.4 per cent of its common variance.

Table 5.2

Perceived Quality of Work-Life (PQWL) of Officials: Means and Standard Deviations

Quality of Work-life	N	Mean	SD	SE	Minimum Score	Maximum Score	95 per cent Conf.	Int. for Mean
Perceived influence in work-life	164	3.03	0.67	0.05	1.00	4.82	2.93	3.13
Perceived level of amenities in/at workplace	150	2.59	0.61	0.05	1.50	4.66	2.50	2.69
Perceived nature of job	164	3.50	0.68	0.05	1.50	4.83	3.40	3.61
Perceived nature of supervisory behaviour/practices	164	3.50	0.71	0.05	1.00	5.00	3.39	3.60
Perceived quality of work-life (composite)	150	12.78	2.06	0.17	7.49	18.82	12.45	13.12

Table 6.3
*Construct Validity and Test Reliability of Measures
of Perceived Quality of Work-Life*
(N = 119)

	Measures				
	Perceived Influence at Work	Perceived Amenities at Work	Perceived Nature of Job	Perceived Nature of Supervisory Behaviour	Perceived Quality of Work-Life (PQWL)
	V–12	V–13	V–14	V–15	NV–1
Validity* Coefficient	.77	.71	.71	.78	.72
Reliability Coefficient+	.89	.75	.84	.91	.77

* h^2 Values
+ derived from analysis of variance

Reliability of Measures

As Table 6.3 shows, each single reliability coefficient was higher than its corresponding validity coefficient, as it should be. Each of the four measures of perceived quality of life was individually highly reliable. These results provided further confirmation of growing information about the trustworthiness and usefulness of these instruments for measuring satisfaction with (or alienation from) the four important aspects of work-life (Mehta and Jain, 1979; Mehta, 1976; Ahmed, 1986). The composite measure of PQWL or work-satisfaction also emerged as highly reliable (.77) suggesting that components and the composite measure can be used for measurement and analysis as per requirements.

Socio-Political Outlook

Measures of misanthropy and sense of political powerlessness (see Appendix III for items) showed high loading on Factor 6 as can be seen from Table 6.4. It clearly indicated a lack of faith in people and in oneself (as far as political matters were concerned). It was designated as authoritarianism of which the most important

Table 6.4
New Variables (Scales) Derived from Factor
Analysis: Factor 6: Authoritarianism
(NV–5)

Variables	Loading on Factor 6	h^2
8 Lack of faith in people	.81	.69
9 Sense of political powerlessness	.62	.66
Other Measures with Significant Loadings on this Factor		
17 Importance of people's participation in development	.26	.56
18 Existing level of people's participation	−.40	.67
25 Employee's job satisfaction	.35	.70
30 Extent to which development information collected	−.23	.58
24 Officers' job satisfaction	.22	.68

component was lack of faith in people, which defined this construct here. It was interesting that the other two measures of socio-political outlook and personality, namely, the sense of political normlessness and conservative-dogmatism, did not show significant loadings on this factor. These two showed high loadings on the same factor as the sense of political powerlessness and misanthropy in earlier studies (Mehta, 1977b; Rao and Mehta, 1978) and they stood out as single important variables by themselves not necessarily associated with authoritarianism as defined here. Earlier the four variables thus had shown loadings on one factor as authoritarianism which was similar to the results reported by Adorno *et al.* (1950) in their classic study of the authoritarian personality. However, the construct identified here as authoritarianism was marked by a lack of faith in people as well in one's own competence to democratically influence the political process. This was, therefore, highly loaded with the sense of political powerlessness. Officials found high on this measure were also not happy with the existing level of people's participation in development and with the extent to which development information was collected. The results, therefore, tended to suggest that this (i.e., athoritarianism or powerlessness) was accompanied by some kind of dissatisfaction with development programmes.

Mean Scores and Standard Errors

Results recorded in Table 6.5 show very low standard errors of the obtained mean scores for the measure of authoritarianism (combination of misanthropy and sense of political powerlessness), conservative–dogmatism and the sense of political normlessness. The obtained central tendencies, therefore, showed good stability and reliability at 95 per cent level of significance.

Table 6.5
Officials' Socio-Political Orientation (Personality): Means and Standard Deviations

Personality Measure	N	Mean Score	SD	SE	Minimum Score	Maximum Score	95 percent Conf.	Int. for Mean
Authoritarianism	119	5.35	1.05	0.10	2.75	7.95	5.16	5.55
Sense of political normlessness	119	3.69	0.77	0.07	1.66	5.33	3.55	3.83
Dogmatism	122	3.74	0.77	0.07	1.50	5.00	3.60	3.87

Reliability and Validity of Measures

Table 6.6 reports reliability and construct validity of the measures of socio-political outlook (personality) and of the combined measure of authoritarianism. It was interesting to note that the single measure of misanthropy appeared to be more reliable than the combined measure of authoritarianism. It was decided to use the single measure as well as the combined measure in subsequent analysis.

Table 6.6
Realiability and Construct Validity of Measures of Socio-Political Outlook (Personality)

	Measures				
	Misanthropy	Sense of Political Powerless-ness	Sense of Political Normless-ness	Conservative Dogmatism	Authori-tarianism
Test-Reliability*	.75	.67	.63	.59	.68
Construct Validity (h²)	.69	.66	.64	.55	.67

* derived from Misanthrophy and Sense of Political Powerlessness

The Organisation Status and Technical Orientation

Three organisational background variables, namely, length of service, years spent on the same (present) job (stagnation), and income along with the respondent's age, showed loadings on Factor 2 as can be seen from Table 6.7. This was an important factor accounting for 8.6 per cent in the common variance of 68 per cent in the factor matrix. In its contribution to the common variance, it was second only to work satisfaction or quality of work-life. It appeared to be the factor of *organisation status* in the traditional sense of length of service based on seniority. High loadings of .91 (length of service) and .85 (age) clearly indicated this construct.

Table 6.7
New Variables (Scales) Derived from Factor Analysis: Factor 2:
Organisation Status (Length of Service)
(NV–2)

Variables	Loading on Factor 2	h^2
2 Age	.85	.81
5 Length of service	.91	.85
6 Years in the same position	.31	.57
7 Income	.57	.74

Other Measures Showing Significant Loadings on this Factor		
16 Evaluation of self-reliance and capability development in rural poor	.30	.67
27 Role of staff associations in promoting participation in administration	−.32	.68
11 Conservative–dogmatism	.23	.55
28 Extent to which EF used in development programmes	.22	.58
30 Extent to which development information is presently collected	.22	.58

Interestingly, organisation status was associated with positive assessment of development performance (self-reliance and internal capability of the poor) and of management (implementation) practices as applied to development programmes (collection of development information and the use of environmental factors in programmes). At the same time, this was characterised by a conservative-dogmatic social outlook. Greater the organisation status (length of service—seniority) greater the social outlook seemed to be conservative and the greater was the orientation for performance justification. We will come back to this point in later analysis and discussion.

Technical Orientation

The personal background variable of technical training/education emerged as a distinct organisation factor (Factor 9) named here as technical background. It showed high construct validity of .74, as can be seen from Table 6.8. It was interesting to note that the technically trained and oriented officials (middle managers) were neither satisfied with the development performance nor with the use of feedback for improving development programmes. They also seemed to show a greater sense of stagnation in their mid-careers. Emergence of technical training as a separate factor as distinct from organisation status was itself an important finding. The two constructs were characterised by opposing bureaucratic tendencies, particularly with regard to performance and use of feedback for improving performance.

Table 6.8
New Variables (Scales) Derived from Factor Analysis:
Factor 9: Technical Orientation
(NV–8)

Variables	Loading on Factor 9	h^2
4 Level of technical training	.79	.74

Other Measures with Significant Loadings on this Factor		
7 Income	.43	.74
16 Self-reliance in rural poor	−.62	.67
31 Extent to which feedback used in programme	−.23	.67
25 Employee's job satisfaction	.24	.70
6 Years in the same position (stagnation)	.24	.57

Twelve Factors

Factor analyses, thus yielded 12 factors in 33 variable matrix, constituting ten constructs (the new variables). These new variables were perceived quality of work-life (PQWL) or Work Satisfaction (NV–1); organisation status (NV–2) six development related bureaucratic orientations (DRBOs), namely, participation orientation (NV–3), performance justification (NV–4), complacency (NV–6), coaching–dependence (NV–7), 'association' orientation and feedback orientation (NV–10), authoritarianism (NV–5) and technical orientation (NV–8). The factor-analytic study also revealed certain characteristics as correlates of some of these constructs, thus helping us to understand their meaning. However, there was a need to further explain variance in the various constructs, particularly the DRBOs and the PQWL and their dimensions in order to obtain a clear picture of the underlying bureaucratic behaviour at the middle management level in government. We turn to them in the following chapters.

7

Variance in Development Related Bureaucratic Orientations

We have briefly discussed the meaning of the various development related bureaucratic orientations in behaviour at the middle management level in government in chapter 6. Results suggested that participation and feedback orientations were inter-related and the remaining four, namely, performance justification, complacency, coaching and association orientations seemed to relate to each other. The first two probably indicated some achievement/ performance oriented tendency and the other four, particularly complacency and justification indicated power and status oriented tendency.

There was, however, a need to pursue the matter further in order to identify significant predictors which could explain the variance in each of these orientations.

BACKGROUND, WORK-LIFE, PERSONALITY AND BUREAUCRATIC ORIENTATIONS: INTER-CORRELATIONS

How are the development related bureaucratic orientations related to the seven background variables, four variables of perceived quality of work-life and the four variables of socio-political outlook and personality? The inter-correlations provide some answers.

Participation Orientation

It was correlated with performance justification and more strongly with perceived supervisory behaviour ($r = .25$, $p<.01$) as well as with faith in people (negative of misanthropy; $r = -.15$, $p<.05$).

Performance Justification

Besides correlating with complacency and association orientations, it seemed to be associated with the sense of political efficacy (opposite of powerlessness; $r = -.18$, p<.01) and acceptance of prevailing political (regime) norms (opposite of the sense of political normlessness; $r = -.18$, p<.05). On the work side, it was associated with perceived influence at work ($r = .15$, p<.05) nature of job ($r = .19$, p<.01). Background-wise, justification orientation was associated with increasing age and the posting of the respondent. Greater the proximity to development work, the higher was the orientation

Sence of Complacency

Like justification, complacency was also associated with the sense of political efficacy and a sense of identification with the regime. Besides nature of job and supervisory behaviour at work, it was strongly associated (all three r significant at .01 level) with the perceived influence in work-life. Like justification, complacency was also associated with increasing age and the official's job location, i.e., proximity to development and field work. Interestingly, the level of education was negatively associated with the sense of complacency ($r = -.20$, P<.01). The correlational analysis seemed to suggest that the sense of complacency (or self-satisfaction) was characterised by an active support to the regime and by satisfaction with the quality of work-life (in the government). It was found more among elder officials and among those located closer to district/block level development work.

Coaching–Dependence Orientation

Besides showing association with feedback orientation, coaching–dependence orientation also showed significant correlations with perceived influence at work and perceived supervisory behaviour. However, the interesting difference was its significant correlation with conservative–dogmatism ($r = .24$, P<.01). This orientation, therefore, appeared to be associated with a socially conservative and dogmatic tendency. Further, it was positive with age and length of service but negative with proximity to development (field) work, indicating that it was associated more with elderly senior officials located higher in the hierarchy—in departments and secretariats. It, therefore, seemed to be hierarchically related, conservative orientation associated with satisfying influence and supervisory behaviour in the work-life. It was not so much job oriented as relationship oriented.

'Association' Orientation

It was associated with both performance justification and feedback orientation, unrelated to any socio-political variables and related to the perceived influence at work, nature of job and perceived supervisory behaviour (interestingly, unrelated to amenities at work) and negatively related to proximity to development work. It seemed that this orientation was not associated with work alienation or dissatisfaction. On the contrary, it was characterised by a sense of satisfaction with the perceived quality of work-life (except amenities) and was found more among the middle level officials posted at departmental headquarters and secretariats.

Feedback Orientation

Like performance justification and complacency, feedback orientation was marked by a sense of political efficacy and support for regime norms. Unlike other orientations, it seemed to be related to satisfaction with work amenities as well as the nature of the job and, interestingly, with the level of education ($r = .19$, $P<.01$).

Inter-Correlation Among New Variables

Ten new variables as obtained in factor-analysis along with the level of education, sense of political normlessness and conservative–dogmatism were inter-correlated.

Interestingly, work-satisfaction (PQWL) was associated with four of the six development related bureaucratic orientations. Performance justification, complacency, coaching and 'association' orientation were marked by a sense of satisfaction with work-life in the government. Does work-satisfaction promote such behavioural orientation to development within the bureaucracy? Does it mean that officials who enjoy and feel satisfied with the quality of their work-life in government show a greater sense of complacency as well as a greater tendency to justify the ongoing performance in development? Do such middle level officials also show greater tendency for coaching and for association? Are they less authoritarian or feel less powerless but show greater dissatisfaction with prevailing regime norms? We will revert to such questions later in the discussion.

While the obtained inter-correlations did explain certain associations and characteristics, the meaning was not very clear because variables were themselves inter-related. It was difficult to say with certainty which one was more important than others in explaining the variance in development related bureaucratic orientations and in work satisfaction. Multiple regression analyses pursued this matter further to reveal the significance of the explained variance and to locate specific predictors of each orientation.

EXPLAINING VARIANCE IN DEVELOPMENT RELATED BUREAUCRATIC ORIENTATIONS

Factor analyses and the subsequent correlational analyses, as mentioned above, revealed certain relationships of variables with each other and with and among the constructs identified as development related bureaucratic orientations. On treating these orientations one by one as dependent variables, their variance was predicted using the rest of the variables as independent. Results of such multiple regression analyses are shown in Tables 7.1 to 7.6. We shall discuss the results one by one in order to understand and explain the meaning of the various components of the obtained variance and to locate significant predictors of each of the six bureaucratic orientations.

Participation Orientation

Twenty independent variables comprising the remaining five bureaucratic orientations, four variables of socio-political outlook (personality), four variables of perceived quality of work-life and the remaining seven variables of organisation and personal background, as seen in Table 7.1, contributed only 17 per cent variance ($R^2 = .17$; $F = 1.00$; ns) in this bureaucratic behaviour which is specified as participation orientation. It was obvious that there were other factors, not known and not included in the present analyses, which accounted for most of the variance in this orientation.

Table 7.1
Multiple Regression Analysis of Variance in Orientation
Supportive of Participation in Development
(NV-3)

Individual Variable	Beta	R^2 Change	Individual Variable	Beta	R^2 Change
V-7	.02	.00	V-12	-.07	.01
NV-4	.17†	.03	V-13	-.01	.00
NV-6	-.14*	.00	V-14	-.07	.00
NV-7	.08	.01	V-15	.32†	.04
NV-9	-.14*	.01	V-1	.00	.00
NV-10	.12	.01	V-2	.09	.00
V-8	-.13	.02	V-3	-.07	.00
V-9	.07	.00	V-4	-.05	.01
V-10	-.03	.00	V-5	-.02	.00
V-11	-.01	.00	V-6	-.12	.01

$R^2 = .17$; $F = 1.00$; ns
* significant at .05 level
† significant at .01 level

However, individual beta values (standard partial regression coefficients) (Kerlinger and Pedhazur 1973, 164–65) revealed some interesting information. Faith in people (opposite of misanthropy) accounted for 2 per cent variance in participation orientation (beta = -.13, ns with misanthropy). This was, however, statistically not significant. Perceived supervisory behaviour and practices at the workplace emerged as a significant predictor (beta = .32, p<.01) of this orientation. None of the other three dimensions of perceived quality of work-life contributed much. None of the background variables emerged as important in this respect. Three of the five bureaucratic orientations individually emerged as significant predictors—one positive and two negative—of participation orientation. Thus, performance justification was a postitive predictor (beta = .17, p<.01) accounting for 3 per cent variance. However, complacency (beta = -.14, p<.05) and 'association' orientation (beta = -.14, p<.05) emerged as negative predictors, not contributing much to the total variance.

Thus, it was clear that faith in people and, more importantly, satisfaction with supervisory behaviour and practices and performance justification orientation tended to significantly boost the bureaucratic orientation supportive of participation. On the other hand, the bureaucratic sense of complacency and the orientation for 'association' tended to significantly hinder and weaken it. Why should the tendency for association weaken and the tendency to justify (and/or defend) current development performance boost participation orientation was not very clear. Probably, it could be explained by the nature of these factors. The factor of 'association' (see Table 5.6) was loaded with a favourable attitude to staff associations and their participation in management in government seemed stronger among secretariat based officials and those favourable to efforts for controlling red-tapism. This orientation was not necessarily a liberal social attitude (as this variable did not show a significant loading on this factor). On the other hand, the factor of participation (see Table 5.2) was a liberal orientation with conservative–dogmatism showing a high negative loading on it, attaching importance to the organisation of rural workers, people's participation and participation of staff in government management. Therefore, these two factors, revealed attitudes negative of each other. On the other hand, the factor of performance justification was loaded with active dissatisfaction with the working environment and amenities and was much more pronounced among officials positioned closer to the field (see Table 5.3). Such officials tended to attach importance to the organisation of rural workers (like those high on orientation for participation). The tendency to justify performance was also associated with the sense of political efficacy as well as anger with the administrative system. Such efficacious anger seemed to boost the orientation desirous of and favourable to participation.

However, the supervisory behaviour and practices at the work place emerged as the most significant positive predictor of the subordinate's orientation supportive of participation. Superiors' respect for subordinates' ideas and appreciation of their work, positive image of subordinates' capability and harmonious and supportive relationship with them (see Appendix II for items) helped shape and promote a liberal participative attitude among the subordinates. In other words, informal and friendly working relationship rather than formalised hierarchical and 'officious' administrative behaviour was conducive to promoting a forward looking and participative, may be democratic, outlook among junior level officials in government organisations.

Performance Justification

Twenty independent variables explained 29 per cent variance ($R^2 = .29$, F = 2.03, P<.05) in the bureaucratic orientation of performance justification, as seen in Table 7.2. Variable-wise, 18 per cent of this variance was explained by the remaining five bureaucratic orientations; 4 per cent by variables of perceived quality of work-life; 5 per cent by the background variables and just 2 per cent by four measures of socio-political outlook.

Table 7.2
Multiple Regression Analysis of Variance in Performance Justification
(NV–4)

Individual Variable	Beta	R^2 Change	Individual Variable	Beta	R^2 Change
NV–3	.15†	.03	V–12	−.04	.00
V–7	−.08	.00	V–13	−.18†	.03
NV–6	.20†	.11	V–14	.05	.00
NV–7	−.03	.00	V–15	.17	.01
NV–9	.17†	.04	V–1	.09	.01
NV–10	−.04	.00	V–2	−.19	.02
V–8	−.02	.00	V–3	.04	.00
V–9	−.15*	.02	V–4	−.01	.00
V–10	−.02	.00	V–5	−.03	.00
V–11	−.00	.00	V–6	.10	.02

$R^2 = .29$; F = 2.03 (significant at .05 level)
* significant at .05 level
† significant at .01 level

Dissatisfaction with Amenities

None of the background variables, however, emerged as significant predictors, not even the variable of position proximity to development which revealed a significant loading on this factor (see Table 5.3). The respondents' age explained 2 per cent variance in this orientation (beta = −.19; ns) which was, however, not a significant predictor by itself. Of the 4 per cent variance due to perceived quality of work-life, 3 per cent was contributed by a dissatisfaction with amenities at the workplace, which was a significant predictor of performance justification (beta = −.18, P<.01). Greater the dissatisfaction with the available facilities and amenities at the workplace and in work-life, higher was the tendency to justify the present development performance practices. The results suggested that this tendency was not related to postings (or as some say, punishment field postings) as such but it seemed to be accompanied by a sense of dissatisfaction with the work environment; with facilities like housing, water, canteen, transport, education, medicine and also with salary etc. When the variable of posting was controlled work dissatisfaction, due to poor work amenities including salary etc., seemed to contribute to the promotion to the tendency to justify performance.

Variance due to other Orientations

Participation orientation explained 3 per cent variance (beta = .15, P<.01); 'association' orientation 4 per cent (beta = .17, P<.01); and complacency as much as 11 per cent variance (beta = .20, P<.01) in the orientation for performance justification. All three were significant positive predictors of this orientation. Interestingly, when other variables were controlled, such middle managers in government who tended to justify (or defend) the current level of development performance and practices were also inclined, at the same time, to support people's participation in development and also their own participation in developmental decision-making (e.g., planning). Their dissatisfaction with work amenities probably promoted in them an 'association' orientation. However, the most important finding was the contribution of the sense of complacency to the variance in performance justification. Greater the sense of complacency, i.e., higher the self-satisfaction with their competence, higher was the tendency for performance justification. Those who thought they were competent and 'prepared' for development tasks were more likely to show a greater tendency to justify performance.

Sense of Political Efficacy

The sense of political powerlessness emerged as a negative predictor (beta = −.15, P<.05) of the orientation for performance justification. Therefore, the tendency to justify performance was, accompanied by a sense of political efficacy. Such officers thought that it was possible and that they were competent to influence politics and political events. At least at the level of thinking, they seemed to be politically active. They were also likely to be political activists as other findings suggest (Mehta, 1977b; Ahmed, 1971; Atal, 1969). Therefore, performance justification was not a passive or indifferent tendency, nor was it a characteristic of docile or inactive officials. On the contrary, it seemed to be associated more with the politically active among them. A sense of political efficacy accompanied by strong dissatisfaction about their own preparedness for development tasks highlighted the fact that this orientation was indicative of the political behaviour of middle level bureaucrats. Such officials were activists, to be found more at district and ground levels.

The Profile

The emerging profile of performance justification seemed to include dissatisfaction with work environment and work-related amenities; 'association' orientation, i.e., given to forming associations and being active in them; politically efficacious, i.e., having a sense of competence and confidence to be able to influence political events; inclined to support people's participation in development and demand their own (self) participation; and a strong sense of complacency, i.e., a sense of self-satisfaction with their own expertise and preparedness for handling jobs and their own involvement in development work. Therefore, it seemed that dissatisfaction with the work environment and amenities coupled with a sense of efficacy and undue self-confidence promoted the orientation for performance justification.

The 20 variables in Table 7.2 explained only 29 per cent variance in performance justification. Obviously there were other important factors which shaped it and contributed to its variance. For example, political leadership (within the government), i.e., the party in power, has a strong tendency to claim and repeatedly publicise achievements in development programmes. This is particularly true for anti-poverty programmes which were the focus of the present study. Hence, such strong defence of achievements and development programmes is replicated at lower levels thus promoting the orientation for performance justification among officials. Any deviation in this regard could be construed as political criticism and could easily be linked to opposition parties. Officials may not like to take such a risk. On the contrary, officials tending to justify performance seemed to be politically active and supporters of the prevailing political system. The behaviour and desires of the higher political leadership only reinforced the tendency at the middle and grassroot levels.

Field evidence (Jain *et al.*, 1985) suggests the existence of strong links between district and higher level development bureaucracy and the rural rich and other vested interests who stand to gain by 'poor' performance in programmes like IRDP, which enable them to corner the funds and other benefits earmarked in such programmes. Self-interest and support of political interest may also reinforce the tendency to justify performance. It is interesting to note that such justification (*essentially defensive* behaviour) tends to be made rather forcefully and actively, maybe even *offensively*. It is another matter that such a bureaucratic orientation becomes an active barrier to efforts for improving development performance and the development process.

Sense of Complacency

Twenty independent variables including the remaining five bureaucratic orientations explained about 33 per cent variance in the sense of complacency, as seen in Table 7.3 (R^2 = .33; F = 2.40 P<.01). One-third of the total variance, i.e., 13 per cent was explained by the five development related bureaucratic orientations; 3 per cent by four measures of socio-political outlook (personality); 6 per cent by four variables of perceived quality of work-life and the remaining about 9 per cent by organisational-personal background variables.

Socio-Political Outlook and PQWL

It was interesting that none of the personality variables and the perceived quality of work-life variables emerged as significant predictors. The sense of political efficacy did contribute 2 per cent variance (beta with political powerlessness = −.13, ns) and perceived influence in work-life and satisfaction with supervisory behaviour respectively explained 3 per cent and 2 per cent variance in complacency. Statistically, these did not come out as significant predictors (beta = .10 and .15 respectively, F values not significant). It seemed that the sense of complacency was characterised by a sense of political efficacy and relational and personal influence satisfaction at the workplace, although not very prominently.

Background Variables
Background variables contributed 9 per cent variance in the sense of complacency and three of these emerged as significant predictors of this orientation as seen in Table 7.3. Thus, respondents'

Table 7.3
Multiple Regression Analysis of Variance in Complacency
(NV–6)

Individual Variable	Beta	R^2 Change	Individual Variable	Beta	R^2 Change
NV–3	−.12*	.00	V–12	.10	.03
NV–4	.20†	.12	V–13	−.10	.00
V–7	.06	.00	V–14	.14	.01
NV–7	.13*	.01	V–15	.15	.02
NV–9	−.07	.00	V–1	.12	.02
NV–10	−.04	.00	V–2	.28†	.01
V–8	.03	.00	V–3	−.22†	.04
V–9	−.13	.02	V–4	.02	.00
V–10	−.03	.01	V–5	−.25†	.02
V–11	−.05	.00	V–6	−.08	.00

R^2 = .33; F = 2.40 (significant at .01 level)
* significant at .05 level
† significant at .01 level

age emerged as a positive predictor (beta = .28, P<.01). Greater the age, higher was the officials' sense of complacency about development work. Younger officials were less complacent than their elder (not necessarily senior) colleagues. However, length of service which ordinarily goes with age showed just the opposite tendency here. When all other factors (including age) were controlled, length of service (experience) emerged as a negative predictor of complacency (beta = −.25, P<.01). It tended to reduce complacency and probably enhance vigilance and maybe carefulness. Education also emerged as a negative predictor (beta = .22, P<.01). The greater the educational level of officials, the lower was their sense of complacency (and greater the sense of vigilance) about development work. Position proximity to development work, i.e., posting closer to the field, made a positive contribution of 2 per cent variance in the sense of complacency though it was not a significant predictor (beta = .12, ns). The results, however, suggested that field officials may be more complacent than others.

Bureaucratic Orientations

As mentioned above, the five development related bureaucratic orientations together contributed 13 per cent variance in the sense of complacency. Interestingly, 12 per cent was explained by the orientation for performance justification alone (beta = .20, P<.01) and the remaining 1 per cent by coaching-dependence orientation (beta = .13, P<.05). The greatest contributor to the government middle managers' sense of complacency about development work was their tendency to justify current performance and practices in development programmes. It should be recalled here that the same was true about performance justification itself where the maximum contribution to its variance was made by a sense of complacency. It was, therefore, very clear that the two orientations were highly inter-related although each one was an independent variable.

Participation orientation was a significant positive predictor in case of performance justification, whereas in the case of complacency it emerged as a negative predictor, although it did not explain any variance (beta = −.12, P<.05). Similarly, coaching orientation was negative to performance justification and positive to complacency. Both were associated positively with the sense of political efficacy. However, in case of performance justification it was more definite. Both of these were also associated with dissatisfaction with work-related amenities, again more definitely in case of performance justification. Both seemed to be associated with satisfaction with supervisory behaviour though not significantly. Thus it was clear that the two were no doubt closely inter-related, but each had its own correlates, sometimes in opposite direction.

The Profile

Since the 20 independent variables included in the study explained only 33 per cent variance in complacency, it was obvious that there were other variables which would account for the remaining variance, maybe in a more important way. We shall come to this point later in the discussion. In the meantime, the profile of the sense of complacency seemed to include performance justification as its strong correlate; coaching–dependence made some contribution; participation orientation weakened it; increasing employee age promoted it, whereas length of service weakened it; education weakened it and it was also somewhat associated with the sense of · political efficacy and satisfaction with supervisory behaviour. It seemed that the older and comparatively less educated and less experienced officials tended to reveal a higher sense of complacency. Among them, those with a greater tendency to justify performance, a greater coaching–dependence orientation and maybe a greater sense of political efficacy with lower participation orientation, showed it more.

Coaching–Dependence Orientation

The independent variables explained only 25 per cent variance in the bureaucratic orientation of coaching–dependence as can be seen from Table 7.4, which was statistically only very marginally

Table 7.4

Multiple Regression Analysis of Variance in Coaching–Dependence Orientation.
(NV–7)

Independent Variables	Beta	R^2 Change	Independent Variables	Beta	R^2 Change
NV–3	.07	.02	V–12	.02	.01
NV–4	−.03	.00	V–13	−.07	.00
NV–6	.14*	.01	V–14	−.08	.00
V–7	−.15*	.01	V–15	.21†	.01
NV–9	.02	.01	V–1	−.21†	.03
NV–10	.17†	.03	V–2	−.08	.01
V–8	.05	.01	V–3	.07	.00
V–9	−.01	.00	V–4	−.09	.00
V–10	.05	.00	V–5	.25†	.02
V–11	.16†	.04	V–6	.10	.01

$R^2 = .25$; $F = 1.63$ (ns)
* significant at .05 level
† significant at .01 level

significant (R^2 = .25; F = 1.63, P<10). Thus, 75 per cent of the variance in this orientation was accountable to other variables which are not directly included here. Of the 25 per cent variance, 8 per cent was contributed by organisation variables; 7 per cent by the five bureaucratic orientations; 5 per cent by socio-political outlook and the remaining about 2 per cent by perceived quality of work-life variables.

Background Variables

Position proximity to development (PPD), i.e., posting closer to development/field work, explained 3 per cent variance in the coaching–dependence orientation, though in the opposite direction (beta = −.21, P<.01). It emerged as a significant negative predictor. This meant that closer the placement of the official to the field, the lower was his tendency to either provide or indulge in coaching of subordinates and/or to seek dependence on such coaching. It seemed that field level officials neither liked to provide 'tutoring' nor to receive it. In other words secretarial or departmental posting further from field work was associated more with this orientation. This was understandable probably in terms of the hierarchical bureaucratic structure. The variable of the length of service also seemed to foster this tendency (beta = .25, P<.01) thus explaining its 2 per cent variance. When other variables were controlled income appeared to be a negative predictor (beta = .15, P<.5) though contributing just 1 per cent variance.

Bureaucratic Orientations

Feedback orientation explained 3 per cent variance in coaching–dependence orientation and emerged as an important positive predictor (beta = .17, P<.01). Association of feedback orientation with coaching probably suggested an element of helpful behaviour in coaching, and dependence here could mean help-seeking behaviour. Participation orientation also contributed a 2 per cent variance but statistically it was not significant (Beta = .07, ns). However, this finding also tended to suggest an element of help-giving, help-seeking behaviour in coaching orientation. The sense of complacency was also a positive predictor of this orientation (beta = .14, P<.05) suggesting that if at all coaching included some desire to help, it was probably complacent help and not directed so much towards development.

Socio-Political Outlook

Conservative–dogmatism emerged as an important positive predictor of coaching–dependence orientation (beta = .16, P<.01).
It explained 4 per cent variance which was the highest contributor
in this analysis. Greater the social conservatism and dogmatism
among officials, greater was the tendency for coaching–dependence.
Political behaviour indices were not at all important vis-a-vis this
orientation. Therefore, this seemed to be a socially conservative
bureaucratic orientation.

Perceived Quality of Work-Life (PQWL)

These variables contributed the least variance, just 2 per cent in
all, in the coaching–dependence orientation. Satisfaction with
supervisory behaviour, i.e., satisfaction with their seniors' treat-
ment and behaviour toward them, alone emerged as a significant
positive predictor of this orientation. It suggested that satisfactory
superior–subordinate relationship in the government work context
fostered the tendency to provide coaching or tutoring and/or to
receive it. Once again it has to be viewed in the context of the
administrative hierarchy.

The profile of the coaching–dependence orientation seemed to
be secretarial and hierarchy based, seniority (length of service)
based, socially conservative and dogmatic in outlook, lower
income oriented, complacent, feedback oriented, and to some
extent participation oriented.

'Association' Orientation

The twenty independent variables explained just 16 per cent
variance in 'association' orientation as can be seen from Table 7.5
($R^2 = .16$; F = .96, ns). It was obvious that one has to look
elsewhere for variables and factors to explain the variance in this
orientation. Of the available variance, 8 per cent was explained by
other bureaucratic orientations; 5 per cent by PQWL variables;
just 1 per cent by background variables and no contribution was
made by the personality variables.

Bureaucratic Orientations

Performance justification explained 4 per cent variance
(beta = .20, P<.01) and emerged as an important positive predictor

of 'association' orientation. Greater the tendency to justify (one's own) performance, higher was the orientation for 'association'. Feedback orientation was another important positive predictor (beta = .14, P<.05) contributing 3 per cent variance. However, participation orientation emerged as a negative predictor (beta = .14, P<−.05) without making any visible contribution to its variance. This suggested that officials who were inclined to support or promote participation in development etc., were not so much inclined to favour associations as understood here.

Table 7.5

Multiple Regression Analysis of Variance in 'Association' Orientation
(NV–9)

Independent Variables	Beta	R^2 Change	Independent Variables	Beta	R^2 Change
NV–3	−.15*	.00	V–12	.13	.03
NV–4	.20†	.04	V–13	−.02	.00
NV–6	−.09	.00	V–14	−.03	.00
NV–7	.03	.01	V–15	.11	.02
V–7	−.06	.00	V–1	−.14	.01
NV–10	.14*	.03	V–2	−.04	.00
V–8	−.03	.00	V–3	−.05	.00
V–9	−.07	.00	V–4	.03	.00
V–10	.00	.00	V–5	−.03	.00
V–11	−.01	.00	V–6	.06	.00

R^2 = .16; F = 0.96: (ns with Df = 20/98)
* significant at .05 level
† significant at .01 level

Perceived Quality of Work-Life

None of the PQWL variables emerged as significant predictors by themselves. However, perceived influence at the workplace contributed 3 per cent variance (to the total of 16 per cent) in 'association' orientation (beta = .13, P<.10). Greater the perceived influence at the workplace, higher seemed to be the orientation for 'association'.

Satisfaction with supervisory behaviour also contributed 2 per cent variance here (beta = .11, ns). The results seemed to suggest that 'association' orientation, as it emerged in the factor analysis in the present study, was explained more by relationships at the workplace rather than by the nature of the job.

The profile of this construct ('association' orientation) was not very clear—only 16 per cent of its variance was explained by the present independent variables. It seemed to be associated positively with performance justification and feedback orientations and negatively with participation orientation. None of the PQWL variables were significant here. However, some contributions were made by perceived influence at the workplace and supervisory behaviour suggesting that it was probably associated with superior-subordinate relationship at the workplace. Interestingly, it was not at all associated with dissatisfaction with work amenities (including salary). The usual belief that such dissatisfaction promotes unionisation was not found true of this behavioural orientation, identified here as 'association'. It was associated much more with perceived performance and feedback orientation. It seemed to exist more among officials posted away from the field area (e.g., secretarial posting; beta $= -.14$, P<.10), who are given to justifying their performance. This orientation, indicative of collective or associative action, was non-participatory and not concerned so much with improving performance and/or working and service conditions. It seemed to typify behaviour of secretariat and headquarter based officials seeking to obtain more influence for themselves in the organisation.

Feedback Orientation

The independent variables explained 23 per cent variance in feedback orientation, as seen in Table 7.6 ($R^2 = .23$, F $= 1.45$, P<.10). Therefore, there were other more important variables accounting for its variance. Of the available variance, 8 per cent was contributed by the remaining five bureaucratic orientations; 6 per cent by PQWL variables; another 3 per cent by background variables and 4 per cent by personality variables.

Bureaucratic Orientations
Coaching–dependence orientation explained 4 per cent variance in feedback orientation (beta $= .18$, P<.01). As explained above, the relationship between feedback and coaching orientations suggested some element of helping behaviour. However, coaching orientation, as discussed before, emerged as socially conservative behaviour whereas feedback orientation was not that conservative.

'Association' orientation also carried some element of 'collective' orientation and of concern for information. It should be recalled that feedback itself emerged as a significant predictor of 'association' orientation (see Table 7.5). It was, therefore, interesting that feedback orientation was associated with 'coaching' and 'association' orientations, which tended to reveal some meaning of these constructs, each carrying some concern for obtaining information. In case of coaching, information could be in form of guidelines; in case of 'association' it could be about functioning of the organisation and other such matters, and in case of feedback, it could be about performance.

Table 7.6

Multiple Regression Analysis of Feedback Orientation in Government Officials
(NV–10)

Independent Variables	Beta	R^2 Change	Independent Variables	Beta	R^2 Change
V–7	.07	.01	V–1	−.06	.00
NV–3	.11	.01	V–2	.25*	.00
NV–4	−.05	.00	V–3	.15*	.01
NV–6	−.05	.00	V–4	.04	.00
NV–7	.18†	.04	V–5	−.26†	.01
NV–9	.14*	.03	V–6	.07	.00
V–8	.09	.00	V–12	−.16	.00
V–9	.05	.02	V–13	.11	.01
V–10	.12	.02	V–14	.31**	.05
V–11	.13	.00	V–15	.12	.00

$R^2 = .23$; F = 1.45, (P<.10; Df = 20/98)
* Significant at .05 level
† Significant at .01 level
** Significant at .001 level

For the first time in the present analysis, nature of job emerged as a significant positive predictor (beta = .31, P<.001). If the nature of job was perceived as challenging, varied, meaningful, autonomous and therefore satisfying, then the orientation for feedback was higher. This interesting association tended to suggest that feedback orientation was a performance related behavioural characteristic. It is noteworthy that performance justification and the sense of complacency showed no relationship with feedback orientation. Participation orientation did contribute 1 per cent variance but was statistically not significant (beta = .11, ns).

Background Variables

Respondents' age emerged as a significant positive predictor (beta = .25, P<.05) of feedback orientation, though without making any contribution to its variance. Education was a positive predictor of the orientation (beta = .15, p<.05). On the contrary, the length of service emerged as a negative predictor contributing 1 per cent variance (beta = .26, P<.01). It seemed that greater the education and shorter the service (i.e., may be junior or direct recruits to various cadres), the higher was the feedback orientation. Therefore, the more educated middle managers in the government seemed to show a greater tendency for feedback and also greater concern for achievement.

Feedback orientation, therefore, seemed to be characterised by a tendency for providing and seeking coaching (or help); for 'association' (or collective approach); and for perceiving jobs as challenging and meaningful. It was found more among the comparatively more educated and newer recruits (not necessarily younger) in the organisation. In absence of information about other variables responsible for the variance in this orientation, its full meaning was not clear. However, it appeared to be an achievement oriented behavioural characteristic.

Not Much Variance Explained

As is evident from the above discussions, the 20 independent variables—mostly subjective in nature—used in the analysis did not explain much variance in any of the six orientations. The variance thus explained ranged between 16 per cent (in the case of 'association' orientation) and 33 per cent (in the case of the sense of complacency). In fact, the variance explained by the variables used in the present study was significant only for two orientations, namely, performance justification and the sense of complacency. Interestingly, these two variables also explained the maximum variance in each other and appeared to be significantly inter-related, although each seemed to be an independent orientation. It was, therefore, clear that there were other, maybe more important, variables responsible for the variance in each bureaucratic orientation being explained here. Variables relating to the nature of the bureaucracy, government organisation and development were likely to be important in explaining variance in the related bureaucratic behaviour. We will briefly take a look at some of these important objective variables in chapter 9.

8

Explaining the Variance in Perceived Quality of Work-Life

As mentioned in chapter 4, four measures were used to obtain data on perceived quality of work-life (PQWL). These were perceived influence in work-life, perceived amenities at work; perceived nature of job and perceived nature of supervisory behaviour. Each variable was a subjective indicator of the quality of work-life suggesting the extent of satisfaction in this respect. How do we explain such subjectively felt quality of work-life at the middle management level in the government? The 20 independent variables which were used for explaining bureaucratic orientations were also used here. However, in the present case, all six bureaucratic orientations and only three PQWL variables (i.e., other than the one being predicted as a dependent variable) were used along with four socio-political outlook (personality) variables and seven background variables in the multiple regression analysis. The obtained results are briefly discussed below.

Perceived Influence in Work-Life

The independent variables explained as much as 60 per cent variance in the perceived influence in work-life as seen in Table 8.1. Interestingly 40 per cent variance was contributed by the remaining three variables of work-life, namely, amenities at workplace, nature of job and supervisory behaviour; 14 per cent was explained by the six development related bureaucratic orientations and 4 per cent was accounted for by variables of socio-political outlook. Background variables contributed no variance at all. Among the three PQWL variables, 15 per cent variance in perceived influence was explained by amenities at the workplace (beta = .15, P<.05); 14 per cent by nature of job (beta = .25,

P<.01) and another 11 per cent by supervisory behaviour (beta = .47, P<.001). Such strong inter-relationships were expected as all four measures of the quality of work-life had earlier shown high loadings on the first principal factor, designated as work satisfaction or perceived quality of work-life (PQWL). Each variable was processed separately to locate its specific meaning and to see how much variance was explained by development related bureaucratic orientations and other variables. It was noteworthy that the perceived influence in work-life could be predicted so strongly by the remaining three companion variables. It seemed that greater the satisfaction with work amenities, greater was the job satisfaction; and greater the satisfaction with supervisory behaviour, greater was the perceived influence in work-life.

Table 8.1
Multiple Regression Analysis of Variance in Influence at Work

Independent Variables	Beta	R^2 Change	Independent Variables	Beta	R^2 Change
NV–3	−.03	.01	V–7	−.07	.00
NV–4	−.02	.02	V–13	.15*	.15
NV–6	.06	.05	V–14	.25†	.14
NV–7	.01	.02	V–15	.47**	.11
NV–9	.06	.04	V–1	−.03	.00
NV–10	−.09	.00	V–2	.00	.00
V–8	.09	.00	V–3	.08	.00
V–9	.00	.01	V–4	−.03	.00
V–10	−.10*	.03	V–5	.07	.00
V–11	.01	.00	V–6	−.06	.00

R^2 = .60; F = 7.31; (significant at .001 level with Df = 20/98)
  * significant at .05 level
  † significant at .01 level
 ** significant at .001 level

Development Related Bureaucratic Orientations

Although bureaucratic orientations explained 14 per cent variance in the perceived influence at work, none of them emerged as significant predictors in this respect. Interestingly, the sense of complacency contributed 5 per cent and 'association' orientation 4 per cent variance, but these did not come up as significant predictors of perceived influence (respectively beta = .06 and .06;

both ns). Performance justification contributed 2 per cent variance and was a non-significant negative correlate. It seemed that the perceived influence in work-life was unrelated to development related bureaucratic orientations, although some of them did explain some of its variance.

Socio-Political Outlook

The four measures of socio-political outlook together explained just 4 per cent variance of which 3 per cent was explained by the acceptance of political/regime norms (beta = $-.10$, with normlessness; P<.05). It was very important that the sense of political normlessness, or its opposite, i.e., acceptance of regime norms and integration with the prevailing political system, emerged as a significant predictor of perceived influence in work-life in a situation where none of the variables except the companion variables of perceived quality of work-life revealed significant relationships with it. Greater the acceptance of the prevailing norms of political functioning, the greater seemed to be the perceived influence at the workplace. Therefore, middle managers who were psychologically part of the political system felt more influential at the workplace.

Background Variables

It was significant that none of the organisational variables such as length of service and posting and personal variables like education explained any variance in the perceived influence at work. They made practically no contribution in this respect.

The Profile

Therefore, the profile of perceived influence in work-life among middle managers in the government suggested that it was highly dependent on/or related to other aspects of the perceived quality of work-life. At least statistically it seemed unrelated to development related bureaucratic orientations as well as to respondents' background. It was associated with an acceptance of political norms. Supporters of the prevailing political culture and regime functioning enjoyed much greater influence at their workplace than the critics. On the other hand, officials with a sense of political normlessness or dissatisfaction with political functioning and culture felt deprived of influence at their workplace.

Theoretically, it was an important finding in as much as political alienation, as indicated by normlessness, seemed to be significantly correlated with work alienation, as indicated by a lack of influence at the workplace.

Amenities at Work

The independent variables explained 44 per cent variance in perceived amenities at workplace, another dimension of perceived quality of worklife as seen in Table 8.2 ($R^2 = .44$; $F = 3.94$;

Table 8.2
Multiple Regression Analysis of Variance in Amenities at Work

Independent Variables	Beta	R^2 Change	Independent Variables	Beta	R^2 Change
NV–3	−.01	.01	V–12	−.21†	.16
NV–4	−.14†	.01	V–7	.12	.01
NV–6	−.08	.00	V–14	.06	.00
NV–7	−.05	.01	V–15	.20†	.02
NV–9	−.02	.02	V–1	−.35**	.08
NV–10	.08	.02	V–2	.24*	.01
V–8	.08	.00	V–3	−.04	.00
V–9	−.23†	.05	V–4	−.10	.01
V–10	.05	.00	V–5	−.14	.01
V–11	.00	.01	V–6	−.07	.00

$R^2 = .44$; $F = 3.94$; (significant at .01 level with Df = 20/98)
* significant at .05 level
† significant at .01 level
** significant at .001 level

P<.01). Unlike perceived influence, the remaining three dimentions of PQWL explained only 18 per cent variance here; another 7 per cent was explained by development related bureaucratic orientations; 6 per cent by socio-political outlook; and as much as 12 per cent (against 0 per cent in the case of influence) variance was explained by background variables.

Other Dimensions of PQWL
Of the 18 per cent variance, 16 per cent alone was explained by perceived influence (beta = .21, P<.01) and another 2 per cent by supervisory behaviour (beta = .20, P<.01). Interestingly, nature

of job made no contribution to this variance and emerged as unrelated to amenities at the workplace. Greater the influence and satisfaction with supervisory behaviour—particularly the former—greater was the satisfaction with work-related amenities. Did it mean that officials who have (or perceive) greater influence at work and have good rapport with supervisors manage to have better work amenities in government organisations?

Background Variables
Of the 12 per cent variance in amenities at the workplace explained by the background variables, 8 per cent was explained by position proximity to development or the officials's nature of posting (beta = −.35, P<.001). Officials posted closer to field work, as in districts and blocks, expressed considerable dissatisfaction with their work amenities. It emerged as the single most important predictor (after perceived influence) of satisfaction with work amenities. The findings here confirmed the well known view that field officials and development workers suffer from a lack of amenities like housing, water, education, recreation, medicine etc. Age also emerged as a positive predictor in this respect (beta = .24, P<.05. It meant that younger officials harboured a greater sense of dissatisfaction with their work amenities.

Bureaucratic Orientations
These orientations explained 7 per cent variance in work amenities, but only one, i.e., performance justification emerged as a significant predictor (beta = −.14, p<.01). Greater the tendency to justify performance, lower was the satisfaction with work amenities. 'Association' orientation emerged as a non-significant negative factor (beta = −.02, ns) contributing 2 per cent variance; feedback orientation also contributed 2 per cent variance but did not emerge as a significant predictor. Lack of relationship between 'association' orientation and perceived work amenities was interesting because it is widely believed that interest (amenities) related grievances activise staff associations.

Socio-Political Outlook
Of the 6 per cent variance in perceived amenities at work explained by socio-political outlook variables, 5 per cent was explained by the sense of political powerlessness (beta = −.23, P<.01). There-

fore, its opposite, i.e., the sense of political efficacy emerged as a significant positive predictor of satisfaction with amenities at the workplace. Here again, there was a significant relationship between political alienation, as indicated by the sense of political power-lessness and work alienation was indicated by dissatisfaction with work amenities. Political behaviour emerged as an important factor in the work-behaviour of government officials in this respect.

The profile of satisfaction with work amenities revealed the following significant correlates: perceived influence at work; satisfying supervisory behaviour; non-field (maybe secretariat) posting; low tendency for performance justification; and sense of political efficacy. Interestingly, a set of power related variables explained a significant component of variance in this interest related bureaucratic behaviour. Politically and work-wise, efficacious officers perceived much greater work amenities than those who felt powerless both politically and with regard to the nature of work. Does it mean that psychologically powerful officers managed to obtain satisfying working and service conditions?

Perceived Nature of Job

The independent variables explained 50 per cent variance in the nature of job as perceived by middle managers in the government and can be seen from Table 8.3 ($R^2 = .50$; $F = 5.00$, $P<.01$). The three PQWL variables explained 23 per cent; six DRBOs 18 per cent; socio-political outlook variables 6 per cent; and the background explained just 2 per cent variance in satisfaction with the nature of job.

The PQWL Variables

Of the 23 per cent variance explained by the PQWL variables, as much as 20 per cent was accounted for by the perceived influence at the workplace (beta = .31, P<.01). The remaining 3 per cent was contributed by satisfaction with supervisory behaviour (beta = .29, P<.01). The greater the perceived influence and the satisfaction with supervisors, the more the jobs were perceived as meaningful, interesting, challenging and varied. It was interesting that power related dimensions of work satisfaction were significantly correlated with achievement related (challenging jobs) components of the workplace.

Table 8.3
Multiple Regression Analysis of Variance in Influence at Work

Independent Variables	Beta	R^2 Change	Independent Variables	Beta	R^2 Change
NV-3	-.04	.01	V-12	.31†	.20
NV-4	.04	.03	V-13	.06	.00
NV-6	.11	.05	V-7	.03	.00
NV-7	-.06	.01	V-15	.29†	.03
NV-9	-.02	.02	V-1	.03	.00
NV-10	.20†	.06	V-2	-.28†	.02
V-8	-.04	.01	V-3	-.00	.00
V-9	-.10	.03	V-4	-.00	.00
V-10	-.04	.02	V-5	.13	.00
V-11	.06	.00	V-6	.05	.00

R^2 = .50; F = 5.00; (significant at .01 level with Df = 20/98)
† significant at .01 level

Development Related Bureaucratic Orientation
Each of the six bureaucratic orientations contributed some variance in the nature of job. Performance justification explained 3 per cent and complacency accounted for 5 per cent variance in the nature of job. However, these did not emerge as significant predictors. Feedback orientation explained 6 per cent variance and was a significant predictor of job satisfaction (beta = .20, P<.01). It was interesting to note that officials with a greater tendency and support for feedback also showed greater job satisfaction which is indicative of an achievement orientation.

Background Variables
None of the background variables made any contribution—except the respondent's age (beta = -.28, P<.01)—to the variance in the perceived nature of job. Younger officials showed greater job satisfaction. It is noteworthy that expanding development jobs in the government seemed to be perceived as challenging and meaningful more by younger officials.

Socio-Political Outlook
These four variables together explained 6 per cent variance in the nature of job—mostly in a negative direction. Thus, the sense of political powerlessness contributed 3 per cent (beta = -.10, ns) and the sense of political normlessness contributed 2 per cent

variance (bcta $= -.04$, ns) in this respect. The directions of these relationships were interesting, although statistically not significant.

The profile of the perceived nature of job showed the following significant correlates: perceived influence at workplace; perceived supervisory behaviour; comparatively younger age group and feedback orientation in development. Thus, decentralisation and informalisation (as shown in supervisory practices) and availability of influence (it may be a function of supervisory practices) at work emerged as significant correlates of job satisfaction. Does it mean that such practices, which allow for flexibility, freedom and responsibility, promote job challenges for subordinates?

Perceived Supervisory Behaviour

The independent variables explained as much as 63 per cent variance in the perceived supervisory behaviour ($R^2 = .63$, $F = 8.54$, $P<.01$) as can be seen from Table 8.4. Of this 33 per

Table 8.4
Multiple Regression Analysis of Variance in Supervisory Behaviour

Independent Variables	Beta	R^2 Change	Independent Variables	Beta	R^2 Change
NV–3	.14†	.06	V–12	.43†	.29
NV–4	.09	.06	V–13	.13†	.02
NV–6	.08	.07	V–14	.21†	.02
NV–7	.10*	.03	V–7	.03	.00
NV–9	.05	.03	V–1	.00	.00
NV–10	−.05	.00	V–2	.16	.00
V–8	−.08	.01	V–3	.01	.00
V–9	−.02	.02	V–4	.05	.00
V–10	−.02	.01	V–5	−.18†	.01
V–11	−.01	.00	V–6	−.01	.00

$R^2 = .63$; $F = 8.54$; (significant at .01 level with Df = 20/98)
* significant at .05 level
† significant at .01 level

cent was contributed by the remaining three PQWL variables; 25 per cent by the six development related bureaucratic orientations; 4 per cent by the socio-political outlook variables and just 1 per cent was explained by the seven background variables.

PQWL Variables

The perceived influence at the workplace explained as much as 29 per cent of the variance in the perceived supervisory behaviour (beta = .43, P<.01) thus emerging as the most important predictor of satisfaction with supervisory behaviour. As mentioned in chapter 4, supervisory behaviour and practices (see Appendix II) included perceptions regarding the degree of centralisation and formalisation prevalent at the workplace. Greater satisfaction indicated perceptions of lower formalisation and higher decentralisation, thus providing greater freedom, autonomy and respect to the subordinates. Therefore, it was not surprising that greater the perceived influence at the workplace, greater was the sense of satisfaction with supervisory behaviour. It was an interesting and meaningful evaluation of supervisory behaviour and practices by the subordinates in a bureaucratic organisation. The same was true with the remaining two variables, i.e., amenities at the workplace and the perceived nature of job. These also appeared as significant predictors of satisfaction with supervisory behaviour (respectively beta = .13 and .21, both P<.01). Higher the satisfaction with available work amenities and higher the job satisfaction, greater was the subordinate's satisfaction with his senior's behaviour and related practices in this respect.

Bureaucratic Orientations

Of the 25 per cent variance explained by the bureaucratic orientations, 7 per cent was contributed by the sense of complacency (beta = .08, ns); 6 per cent by performance justification (beta = .09, ns) and 3 per cent was accounted for by association orientation (beta = .05, ns). However, none of these appeared to be significant predictors of the perceived supervisory behaviour. Participation orientation explained 6 per cent variance (beta = .14, P<.01) and coaching–dependence contributed 3 per cent variance (beta = .10, P<.05) in this respect and emerged as significant contributors to the variance in satisfaction with supervisory behaviour. The greater the participation orientation and the tendency for giving and taking coaching (maybe help), the higher was the middle managers' satisfaction with behaviour and related supervisory practices of senior officers. It was interesting, therefore, that senior officials' bureaucratic behavioural orientations ·elating to development work appeared to contribute substantially to the variance in subordinates' sense of satisfaction with their supervisors at the same workplace. Does it mean that informal and respectful supervisory behaviour (and practices) promote participation and coaching (help) orientations in their subordinates?

Socio-Political Outlook and Background Variables

The socio-political variables, contributing just 4 per cent variance, did not appear to show any significant relationship with the perceived supervisory behaviour. The same was more true of the background variables where only the length of service (beta = $-.18$, P<.01) showed a significant negative relationship. Higher the seniority (as per the length of service) of middle level officials, lower was their satisfaction with their superior officers. This interesting finding suggested that longer serving officials, not necessarily older in age (beta = .16, ns), showed a sense of dissatisfaction with the behaviour of their seniors. In the prevailing administrative structure, directly recruited officials (like IAS and state administrative services) become superior officers or bosses of promotees and longer serving subordinates. Interestingly, these findings provided empirical evidence in support of the oft-repeated statement that promotees and other similar middle and lower level officials harboured a sense of dissatisfaction with the behaviour of their seniors. A macro-level structural variable was directly reflected in the micro-level behavioural variable.

The profile of perceived supervisory behaviour included the following important and significant correlates: three companion variables of PQWL; participation and coaching orientations; and length of service in the reverse direction. Comparatively newly inducted officials with a participation and coaching orientation showed greater satisfaction with such supervisory practices as were designed to reduce formalisation and centralisation. On the other hand, longer serving officials, not necessarily older (maybe promotees), exhibited a sense of dissatisfaction with their seniors in this respect. Supervisory behaviour emerged as a very important factor in the government's bureaucratic work organisation.

Work Satisfaction: Composite PQWL

As discussed before, four measures of the perceived quality of work-life showed high loadings on the first principal factor designated as work satisfaction or the composite PQWL. The independent variables, consisting of seven background variables, three socio-political variables and six bureaucratic orientations explained 35 per cent variance in work satisfaction ($R^2 = .35$, $F = 3.37$, P<.01) as can be seen from Table 8.5. The bureaucratic orientations explained 13 per cent variance, socio-political variables 12 per cent and the background variables contributed 8 per cent variance in the composite PQWL.

Table 8.5
Multiple Regression Analysis of Variance in Perceived Quality of Work-life (composite PQWL)

Independent Variables	Beta	R^2 Change	Independent Variables	Beta	R^2 Change
NV–10	.07	.04	NV–5	−.43†	.07
NV–1	−.26*	.04	V–10	−.18†	.04
NV–2	.14	.00	V–11	.09	.01
NV–3	.10	.01	NV–3	.09	.00
NV–4	−.04	.00	NV–4	.03	.01
NV–5	.14	.01	NV–6	.26*	.06
V–6	−.10	.02	NV–7	.07	.00
V–7	.07	.00	NV–9	.13	.02

$R^2 = .35$; $F = 3.37$; (Df = 16/102, p. 01)
† significant at .01 level
* significant at .001 level

Bureaucratic Orientations
Of the 35 per cent variance, about one-third, i.e., 13 per cent, was contributed by development oriented bureaucratic orientations. Feedback orientation explained 4 per cent variance, 'Association' orientation and performance justification respectively contributed 2 per cent and 1 per cent variance in work satisfaction. However, none of these beta values were significant. The sense of complacency alone emerged as a significant predictor (beta = .26, P<.001) of the middle manager's work satisfaction as indicated by the perceived quality of work-life and thus explained its 6 per cent variance. A sense of self-satisfaction (complacency) about their own preparedness and expertise for handling expanding development jobs appeared as a very significant factor in middle managers' satisfaction with the prevailing quality of work-life in the government. Greater such self-satisfaction, i.e., complacency about

themselves, the greater was their sense of work satisfaction. It also meant that officials who were vigilant about development requirements in terms of expertise and preparedness and who were critical about their own role perceived shortcomings in the prevailing quality of work-life in governmental organisations.

Work Dissatisfaction: A Positive Factor

It was interesting to note that the most satisfied officials in government organisations were those who were at the same time complacent and not much concerned about developmental work. In this sense, a certain amount of dissatisfaction with the quality of work-life in government organisations and with the structure and nature of its functioning indicated a sense of vigilance in them. Therefore, such dissatisfaction was a positive factor for development work. The responses of senior officials, as discussed in chapter 3, corroborated these finding. They repeatedly stressed the need for raising work morale and motivation and enhancing concern for development within the bureaucracy as a whole by promoting greater decentralisation in administration and by providing challenges on the job and by improving working conditions at the ground level.

Socio-Political Outlook and Personality

As mentioned above, socio-political outlook and personality variables explained 12 per cent variance in the composite perceived quality of work-life (PQWL) or work satisfaction. Of this, 7 per cent accounted for powerlessness/authoritarianism (beta = $-.14$, P<.01) and another 4 per cent by the sense of political normlessness (beta = $-.18$, P<.01). Both these appeared as significant negative predictors of middle managers' sense of work satisfaction in the government. In other words, democratism (opposite of authoritarianism), i.e., faith in people and faith in ones' own political competence, enhanced satisfaction with the perceived quality of work-life. Similarly, acceptance of and integration with prevailing norms of the political system also appeared as significant contributors to the variance in work satisfaction.

These findings were very striking and firmly established the relationship between political alienation and work alienation, and confirmed the findings reported in chapter 6. The feeling of alienation with the wider socio-political environment seemed to be carried into the workplace, promoting similar feelings of alienation with and at the work situation. This was true of the reverse and positive direction. Politically efficacious and pro-anthropic democratically oriented officials tended to perceive their quality of work-life in a much better light thus showing greater satisfaction in this regard. A sense of closeness with the political system also seemed to enhance work satisfaction. Thus, a very significant interface between work and politics in the middle level bureaucracy seemed to emerge here.

Background Variables

The organisation and personal background variables explained 8 per cent variance in work satisfaction of which 2 per cent was contributed by stagnation (beta = .10, ns) and 1 per cent by length of service (beta = $-.14$, ns). None of them appeared as significant predictors in this respect. Position proximity to development, i.e., posting closer to development and field work, explained 4 per cent variance in work satisfaction (beta = $-.26$, P<.001) and emerged as its very significant negative predictor. The closer the posting was to the field, the greater was the officials' sense of dissatisfaction with their work-life.

The findings confirmed the well-known view in this regard that development officials in the field (maybe at district and block levels) were a highly dissatisfied lot. They tended to perceive their quality of work-life as poor and exhibited clear feelings of work alienation. Such alienation and dissatisfaction tended to decrease as officials moved away from development and field work in their postings. Therefore, it is no wonder that some jobs are regarded as reward and others as punishment postings. It was indeed an ironical situation that field postings, so essential for development work, were regarded as punishment postings and officials tended to get alienated from the work itself.

Therefore, the profile of work satisfaction included the following significant correlates: sense of complacency or sense of self-satisfaction with one's own competence; democratism (faith in people and sense of political efficacy); acceptance of norms of the regime and secretariat postings. Officials fortunate enough to be away from the field and posted at headquarters who felt closely aligned with the regime, who were democratically oriented in the sense that they felt efficacious and were not misanthropic and who were complacent about their own expertise and preparedness for development work, were the bureaucrats most satisfied with their quality of work-life. On the other hand, politically efficacious middle managers posted closer to field work and closely aligned with the prevailing political system felt highly alienated from their work situation. Field postings seemed to make all the difference. The result also suggested that there was no linear relationship between perceived quality of work-life and concern for development performance. Comfortable (maybe lucrative) postings in government employment may promote satisfaction with the quality of work-life and at the same time lull officials into complacency, thus retarding efforts for achieving the stated development goals.

9

Administrative Structure, Posting and Bureaucratic Behaviour

Posting occupies a very important place in government service in India. Often transfers to the district and block levels are considered to be punishment postings. Many a times, employees are transferred to what is called a 'punishment posting' in remote areas. Government employees, therefore, try hard to get transferred to urban and metropolitan areas. A recent committee on administrative arrangements for rural development and anti-poverty programmes (Govt. of India, 1985) has made a strong recommendation for a radical restructuring of district administration and to grant special allowances and other amenities in order to attract talent to rural areas. Similar recommendations have been made from time to time by several expert and administrative committees. However, district administration has continued to function in the same colonial style, if not worse, over the last several decades (Jain *et al.*, 1985).

Posting

Over the years, some sort of preference ranking of posts has developed. Barring a few idiosyncratic preferences (such as nearness to place of origin), many of the preferences have come to be shared. Everyone prefers postings in towns with good schools, hospitals, clean drinking water and transport facilities to one in remote and backward areas (other things being equal). Officers, we will assume, prefer a post where a large amount of illicit revenue can be raised over one where opportunities are limited (Wade, 1985: 468–69). Posting, therefore, is an important structural variable, more so now in the context of the increasing number of development programmes. It is an important and active component of the present administrative structure which has been described as an 'exploitative, inegalitarian and oppressive system' (Govt. of India, 1985: 5).

Position Proximity to Development

There are secretariat postings, headquarter (departmental) postings, subordinate office postings, district, block and village level postings. Management related variables of rural development and anti-poverty programmes were the focal points in the present study. By their very nature, these programmes have to be executed in rural and remote areas. Postings at district and block/tehsil levels are, therefore, physically closer to such development programmes than secretariat and department–headquarter postings. Even within the secretariat, some positions are related more to development programmes than others. For example, officers posted in education and public health departments are comparatively closer to development work than those posted in the excise department. As mentioned in chapter 4, the respondents in the present study supplied information about their position, department and actual place of posting. Using such organisational information, they were classified in four groups, on a four point scale, from very remote to development (1) to very close or closest to development (4). Thus, all respondents were rated on this four point scale. This structural variable was then used for analysing intermediate level officers' organisational (bureaucratic) behaviour.

Position Proximity to Development (PPD) Scale

Not only physical proximity (i.e., location of posting) but also the content and nature of their work was taken into consideration in determining their position on the PPD scale. Thus, an educationist posted as inspector of schools, or in a similar position, at state headquarters of the department was rated as 3 on the scale, while an official dealing with education, say assistant secretary in the secretariat, was rated as 2 on the scale. Other secretariat/department postings—such as, in accounts, exise and prisons—at state, central and department headquarters were rated as 1 on the scale. All district postings were rated as 3, unless the incumbents were required to be directly concerned with the implementation of development work such as animal husbandary, agriculture etc., (mostly located at block level) in which case they were rated as 4 on the scale. In the present case, all block level postings came to be rated as 4 on the scale.

Some Examples of Position Proximity

Some examples of actual posting and nature of work will clarify this point. Officials working as experts in animal husbandary, fisheries, agriculture, education, public health, cooperatives, food etc., and directly appointed on such posts and posted at district/ block level were rated as 4 on the PPD scale, i.e., as closest to development. Their counterparts, who were also experts, but were posted on deputation from their respective departments, for example, to the district rural development authority (DRDA), were rated 3, i.e., close to development. Other officials working in the district development departments were rated as 3 and those posted at block level were rated as 4. Officials/experts posted at departmental headquarters, directly concerned with development subjects like fisheries etc., were also rated as 3. Those engaged in mere administrative work (or file work) either at department headquarters or at the secretariat level were rated as either 2 (remote) or 1 (very remote) depending on the nature of their work.

Many of those rated as 4 happened to be the subject matter experts. Some of them were also generalists, but were supposed to be directly involved with development work. Those rated as 3 also included experts mostly on deputation to the DRDA or posted at headquarters. Those rated as 2 and 1 were not only physically remote to development programmes but were also engaged in mostly administrative work, or in some other work not directly related to development.

Organisation Status (Length of Service) and Position Proximity to Development

As mentioned above, position proximity to development (PPD) was determined on the basis of physical proximity to development and nature of work and not necessarily on the basis of length of service and organisation status. As the results in Figure 9.1 show, status as derived from factor-analysis (see Table 5.4 in chapter 5) showed a U-type relationship with PPD ($F = 2.64$, $P<.05$). Those

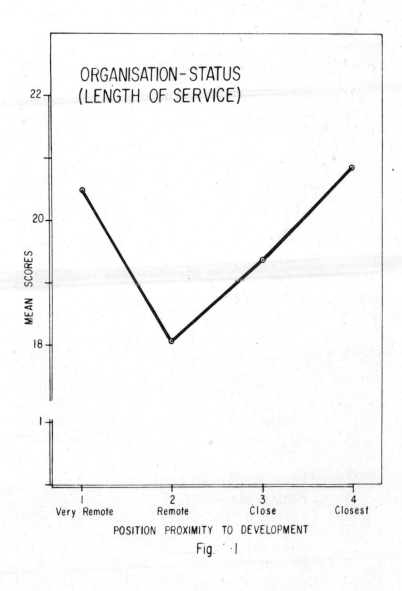

Fig. 1

placed very remote as well as those placed closest to development showed higher organisation-status (length of service, age) than those placed in between—middle level government officials posted at department headquarters and/or on similar remote positions— who seemed to show the lowest organisation-status (i.e., shortest service and the youngest). Those placed at the block level and/or in similar positions closest to development work revealed the highest organisation-status (i.e., longest length of service and the oldest). Keeping this in mind, officials posted closest to development could have an image of being the 'senior-most' in the organisation and may harbour feelings which go with such 'seniority' while, in fact, their actual seniors and bosses were likely to be younger with a shorter length of service to their credit. The latter may be direct recruits to various administrative and other services including the IAS. A conflicting situation was therefore built into the organisation structure.

Position Proximity to Development and Bureaucratic Orientations

The Perceived Quality of Work-Life

The composite perceived quality of work-life or work satisfaction revealed a gradual decline with an increasing proximity to development (F = 2.56, P<.05). As discussed in chapter 8, with other variables controlled, position proximity to development revealed a highly significant negative correlation (beta = −.26, P<.001) with composite perceived quality of work-life. Figure 9.2 expressed it clearly—greater the proximity to development, lower was the quality of work-life and the work satisfaction. It was an important finding which depicted the bureaucratic hierarchy, psychologically. Although PPD was not strictly based on the organisation chart, it seemed to indicate a hierarchy of PQWL and work satisfaction. The further the official was from development work, the more satisfied he was with the quality of his work-life. Therefore, a question naturally arises, as to why should an official welcome a field posting closest to development (mostly in rural areas) where he has to suffer a highly dissatisfying work-life? Another interesting feature of the finding here was that departmental postings (mostly experts) were also associated with the perception of lower quality of work-life than secretariat postings.

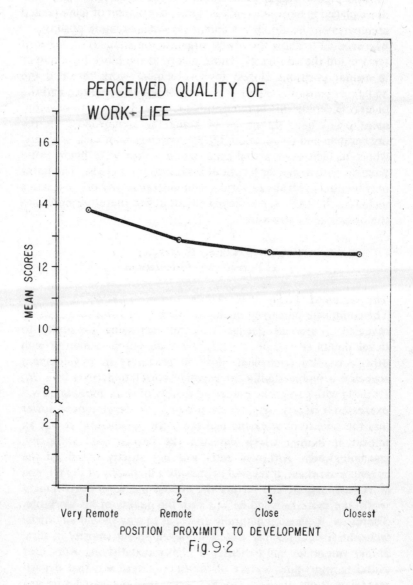

Fig. 9·2

A subjective hierarchy seemed to emerge, corresponding to objective organisation chart, informed by work-values, motivation and social prestige. Low work-motivation for development seemed to be in-built in the organisation structure and bureaucratic hierarchy.

Amenities at Work

The findings shown in Figure 9.2 were very forcefully confirmed by those shown in Figure 9.3. The perceived quality of work amenities, which included housing, education for children, drinking water facilities and salary etc., gradually declined as one moved closer to development work (F = 7.92, P<.001). The result left no room for doubt that development officials were highly dissatisfied in this respect. Their work alienation in this regard surfaced very definitely. The finding provided strong empirical and behavioural confirmation for the concept of punishment posting mentioned above.

Therefore, it was no wonder that work alienation was much greater and work motivation much lower among development officials. The closer they were to development programmes, the more alienated from work and dissatisfied they were. They harboured strong grievances which could only wean them away from much needed development and the anti-poverty programmes. It was quite clear that they had no pride in their work. It did not provide them with the sense of internal satisfaction. They were estranged from their work-life.

Authoritarian Orientation

Interestingly, estrangement from work-life did not particularly weaken development officials' democratic orientation. The middle managers in the government were more or less equally authoritarian or democratic as defined here, irrespective to the PPD (F = 1.20, ns) as can be seen from Table 9.1. This was also confirmed by the regression analysis. With other variables controlled, PPD practically showed no relationship with authoritarianism (i.e., sense of political powerlessness combined with lack of faith in people; beta = 00).

The picture, however, changed when single variables of misanthropy, sense of political powerlessness and sense of political normlessness were considered. Thus yielding some interesting and

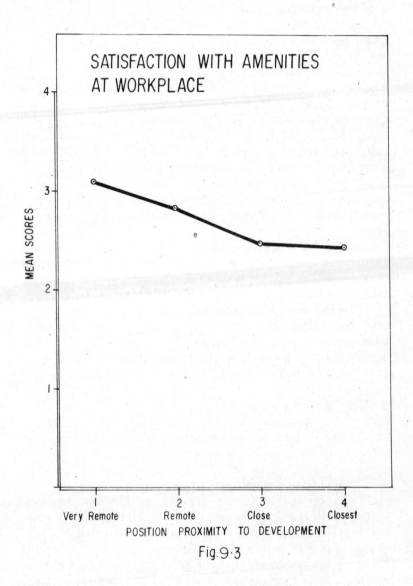

Fig. 9·3

Table 9.1

Means and Standard Deviations in Authoritarianism by Position Proximity to Development

Position Proximity to Development	N	Mean Score	SD	SE	Minimum Score	Maximum Score	95 per cent Conf.	Int. for Mean
1 Very Remote	21	5.43	.86	.19	4.25	6.66	5.03	5.82
2 Remote	16	5.09	.97	.24	3.37	6.75	4.58	5.60
3 Close	46	5.55	1.23	.18	2.75	7.95	5.18	5.92
4 Closest	39	5.20	.91	.15	3.00	6.70	4.90	5.49
Total	122	5.36	1.05	.09	2.75	7.95	5.17	5.54

F = 1.20, ns.

important information. The PPD showed significant correlation (beta = .15, P<.05) with misanthropy (lack of faith in people). Nearer the posting to development and field work (therefore physically closer to people), the lower was the officers' faith in people (whom they were supposed to serve). However, the picture was reversed in the case of political powerlessness and normlessness. Nearer the posting to development, lower was the sense of political powerlessness (beta = −.13, P<.05) as well as the sense of political normlessness (beta = −.18, P<.01).

Greater Sense of Political Efficacy and Greater Acceptance of Regime Norms

The findings clearly indicated that closer the placement of the middle managers to development and field programmes, the higher was their sense of political efficacy and stronger was their acceptance of the prevailing regime norms (of the ruling party). They not only felt much more competent and confident of influencing political events such as elections, but also felt integrated (insiders) with the political culture of the ruling party. It was interesting that while work alienation and political alienation appeared interrelated as discussed in chapter 7, government's field-development officials, seemed to provide an exception to this proposition. They seemed to be significantly alienated from *work* (probably due mainly to lack of work amenities) and closely integrated with the *political system*. However, their lack of faith in people seemed to go together with their lack of work satisfaction. They were actively interested neither in work nor in people, as in the prevailing culture of the political system. They were probably serving the interests of the political system (and their own) than those of the development programmes.

Performance Justification

The tendency to justify present development performance tended to increase with increasing closeness to development programmes as can be seen from Figure 9.4 (F = 3.09, P<.03). This significant relationship seemed to confirm the view that the work alienated middle managers of field-development work tended to defend and justify their poor performance instead of showing readiness for critical self-appraisal and concern for improvement. The lowest orientation for performance justification (therefore maybe greater

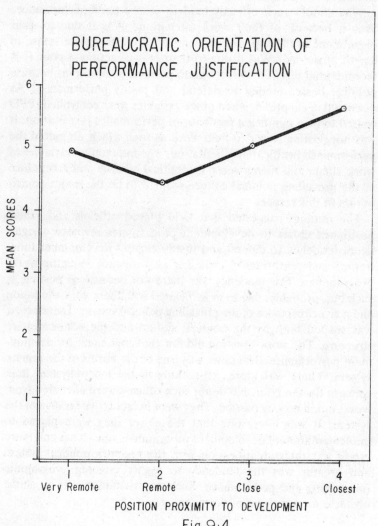

Fig. 9·4

readiness for self-appraisal) was seen among officials placed probably in department headquarters and the highest was found among those placed closest to development, probably the district and block level experts and officials.

Why should such officials tend to justify poor performance? Was it because of their work alienation? Was it due to their resentment of the superior officers to whom they were senior in length of service? Was it due to their fear of getting a poor C R (confidential report)? Was it due to political compulsions because political bosses tended to defend and justify performance? As discussed in chapter 6, when other variables were controlled, PPD ceased to be a significant predictor of performance justification. It was not posting closer to field work as such which promoted the performance justification orientation. The intervening variables of work alienation, higher sense of political efficacy and acceptance of the prevailing political culture seemed to be the major contributors in this respect.

The findings suggested that field placed officials and others positioned closer to development programmes revealed a significant tendency to defend and justify current development functioning and performance including performance in anti-poverty programmes. This tendency was there not because of posting as such but, probably, due to or associated with their work alienation and active acceptance of the prevailing political system. Therefore, it was shaped both by the political system and the administrative structure. The work situation did not challenge them for development performance. The same was true of the norms of the regime system. There was more self-seeking in the macro-system than concern for the poor. No doubt such officers were alienated from work, but in no way passive. They were in fact *active insiders* of the system. It was interesting that the closer they were placed to implementation of development programmes, the closer and more active was their identification with the regime's political system and greater was the tendency to justify ongoing programme functioning and performance. Such an orientation was an active obstacle to improving performance.

Sense of Complacency

The sense of complacency also tended to increase with increasing closeness to development work as seen in Figure 9.5 (F = 3.50,

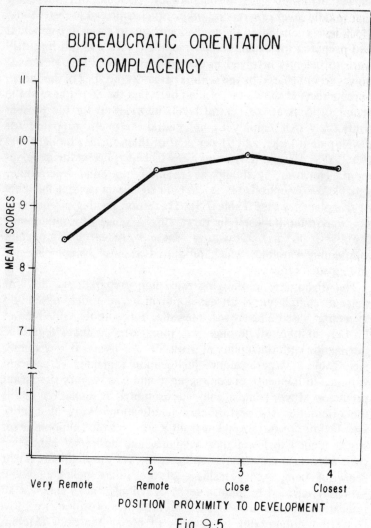

Fig. 9·5

P<.02). Officials placed closer to the field, mostly at district and block levels, were significantly more complacent than those placed in department headquarters and the secretariat. In fact the latter showed the lowest sense of complacency. Therefore, it is interesting that middle level experts and other officials placed at district and block levels considered themselves sufficiently trained, competent and prepared for expanding development jobs and felt that they were sufficiently involved in development work. This view was, however, not shared by the seniors placed at the apex of the Indian bureaucracy. It should be recalled here that the 86 per cent of the senior officials at the central level, interviewed for the present study, felt that employees in general were not prepared for development tasks, and 91 per cent of them further thought that (see Table 3.3 and 3.4) employees lacked concern for development. However, it should be recalled here that when other variables were controlled PPD was not a significant factor in the sense of complacency (see Table 7.3). Therefore, posting as such was not important by itself in promoting a sense of complacency (beta = −.06, ns). Obviously, there were certain important intervening variables which promoted a sense of complacency among such officers.

The dichotomy in thinking regarding preparedness, etc. (or sense of complacency) for development between field based and secretariat based officials was interesting for more than one reason. Earlier, another dichotomy was found among them regarding satisfaction with the quality of work-life. As discussed in chapter 7 (see Table 7.3) performance justification explained 12 per cent variance in the sense of complacency and was its very significant predictor. Maybe complacency was promoted by similar reasons as the orientation for performance justification. Work alienation, i.e., feelings of estrangement from work, was the common factor which tended to lower their vigilance and desire for enhancing their expertise, competence and concern for development. Their sense of being active insiders of the ruling political system probably instilled in them a sense of complacency. This was an indication of their low social achievement motivation, i.e., low concern for improving the quality of life of the poor (Mehta, 1982). A greater tendency for justifying ongoing performance accompanied by a greater sense of complacency among field based officials (as compared to remotely placed secretariat based officials) indicated their low motivation for poverty alleviation programmes. Such behavioural characteristics were ironical as motivation for development was the weakest where it was required the most. Interaction of two important structural variables, namely, the work organisation and the political system, seemed to shape such orientations among field level officials. Their feeling about their organisation status (seniority), as mentioned above, might have also contributed to this process.

Coaching–Dependence Orientation

Unlike performance justification and the sense of complacency, the orientation for coaching–dependence tended to decrease with increasing closeness to development, as can be seen from Figure 9.6 (F = 2.79, P<.04). Greater the PPD, lower was the tendency to seek coaching from seniors and also, probably, to give it. This was confirmed by the regression analysis, as discussed in chapter 7 (see Table 7.4) where PPD emerged as a negative predictor of coaching–dependence orientation (beta = $-.21$, P<.01). The lowest tendency to perceive coaching as important was visible among those placed closest to development (i.e., at the field level). In the government set up, such coaching (or 'help') is given in the form of instructions, guidelines and a plethora of circulars. As one experienced development administrator, chairman of a DRDA, has put it (quoted in Jain *et al.*, 1985; 177) 'the number of instructions, procedures, form norms, amendments, and modifications in every scheme are beyond comprehension of the project officer responsible for implementation of the IRDP scheme . . . '. It was obvious that such coaching from the headoffice or the centre and from their own senior officers was not liked by the development officials posted in the field.

There was again a dichotomy between officials (seniors) placed away from development and those (juniors) placed closer to development. The departmental officials and those in the secretariats revealed an orientation (fondness) for providing coaching and guidelines to their field placed juniors, and in turn receiving such guidance from their seniors. However the 'juniors' placed at the district level did not perceive this as important and did not like it.

The Seniors' Role: As mentioned in chapter 5, an important variable which revealed a very high loading on this factor of coaching–

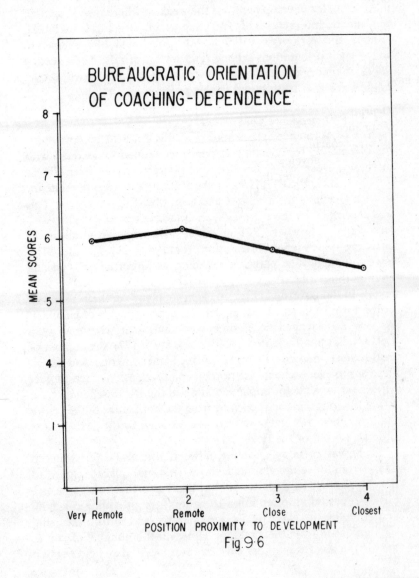

Fig. 9·6

dependence was the perceived importance of seniors' role in developing preparedness and expertise in subordinates. Response to this variable was separately analysed by the PPD. The perceived importance of seniors' role in this respect clearly tended to decrease with the increasing proximity to development ($F = 3.28$, $P<.02$). The multiple regression analysis also identified the PPD as a significant negative predictor of this variable (beta $= -.18$, $P<.01$), accounting for its 6 per cent variance. Therefore, it was clear and beyond any doubt that the closer middle level officials' were placed to development, the less importance they attached to the seniors' role in developing preparedness in subordinates.

This finding was important because it indicated that in the rigid hierarchy ridden government bureaucracy those placed lower in the pyramid but closer to the field did not consider their seniors' role as important in developing them and their expertise. Psychologically, juniors in the field tended to reject the superior role of the seniors in department headquarters and the secretariat at least in this respect. They tended to say to their seniors, 'we do not need your coaching (instructions)' or that 'you are not capable of helping us'.

The field officials' denial of the importance of the seniors' role in developing them also indicates their scepticism of receiving any help from their seniors even at the level of district administration. The bureaucratic rigidities have grown to such an extent that even outside professional help was not welcome, as was found in an action research case study (Mathur and Gupta, 1982). It was found that whenever and wherever a cell wanted to go alone, even if the intervention itself had great merit, the authorities did not allow that effort to be sustained. The bureaucratic ethos at the district level did not allow it to progress or to be repeated because it did not consider such a strategy conducive to its own interests.

Therefore, results here tended to suggest several things. Due to bureaucratic rigidities and ethos juniors, particularly ground level development officials, did not expect any help from their seniors in enhancing their expertise; they did not consider it (coaching through instructions etc.) as important or even necessary for developing their preparedness; they might even think that they did not need any such help. The findings suggested some sort of discontinuity in the bureaucratic structure. The field level officials did not seem to look up for guidance/help. In this respect, they did not seem to belong to the work-organisation. They probably 'looked out' to the political system for help and guidance. It seems political leadership was more important to them than the bureau-cratic leadership.

The politically efficacious field level officers, who felt like *insiders* in the prevailing regime system, who felt complacently satisfied with their own development competence and who tended to strongly defend and justify development functioning and per-formance, saw no need for 'coaching' from their seniors in the bureaucracy. They also showed no need for providing similar coaching to their juniors.

Participation and Feedback Orientations

The PPD showed no variation in bureaucratic behaviour in respect to development participation and feedback ($F = 0.24$, and 1.17; beta = 00 and $-.06$ respectively, both insignificant). The admini-strative structure made no difference in this respect. The fact that closer the placement to development, the closer could be the contact with people and development programmes made no difference in the behaviour of district and field based officers in this respect. Their orientations for participation and feedback were more or less similar to those of their counterparts or seniors in development headquarters and the secretariat.

'Association' Orientation

There was also no clear difference in 'association' related behaviour by PPD ($F = 1.32$, ns). However, with other variables controlled it showed up somewhat greater in those placed away from development (beta = $-.14$, $P < .10$). It was interesting that officials closer to development showed intense dissatisfaction with their interest related work-amenities, but showed lower flexibility in administration matters as compared to those placed higher up. Was it because of their closeness to the political system and their greater acceptance of the norms of the prevailing political culture?

Field Officials' Political and Work Behaviour

These findings suggested an important relationship between middle level officials' political and work behaviour. This relation-ship was much more definitive on the ground level. The following

Table 9.2

Means and Standard Deviations of Perceived Importance of Seniors' Role in Developing Staff Preparedness by Position Proximity to Development

Position Proximity to Development	N	Mean Score	SD	SE	Minimum Score	Maximum Score	95 per cent Conf.	Int. for Mean
1 Very Remote	21	3.67	.48	.10	3.00	4.00	3.45	3.89
2 Remote	16	3.75	.45	.11	3.00	4.00	3.51	3.99
3 Close	63	3.59	.56	.07	2.00	4.00	3.45	3.73
4 Closest	50	3.30	.81	.11	1.00	4.00	3.07	3.53
Total	150	3.52	.65	.05	1.00	4.00	3.41	3.62

F = 3.28, P<.02

pattern seemed to emerge: (a) Critics of the regime felt more deprived of power and influence at work as compared to the regime supporters. (b) However, this general priniciple was not applicable at the field level where active supporters of the regime felt highly alienated from their workplace, more particularly from their service and working conditions. (c) Such work-alienated officials did not depend or seek guidance/coaching of their seniors. They were also not so much inclined to give guidance to their subordinates. Further, they were not too integrated with thier work organisation. On the other hand, they seemed to be involved and integrated more with the prevailing political culture. (d) In their work behaviour, they revealed important characteristics of the prevailing political culture, namely, the tendency to defend and justify performance and the tendency to be complacent about their competence and preparedness. Such officials were, therefore, motivated more by political considerations (may be self-interest) than by challenges of managing and implementing poverty alleviation programmes. (e) Interestingly, secretariat based officials and those placed remotely from the field, expressed much greater satisfaction with their work situation; lower tendency to justify performance, lower complacency, greater coaching orientation and revealed greater administrative flexibility and collecitve action orientation than those placed on the ground.

Field officials entrusted with the task of implementing and managing rural development programmes on the ground were not motivated by a desire to improve their competence, improve the quality of life of the poor, seek feedback from people and promote their participation in order to improve development performance. They were highly dissatisfied with their work situation and sought power through the political system. In this sense, their work-behaviour was highly politicised.

The findings seem to yield a behavioural manifestation of some structural problems of management of development, about which committees and commissions have been reporting (and recommending) from time to time. The British evolved and implemented a system of administration primarily to keep the unorganised rural people under subjugation and for exploiting the natural and human resources for the benefit of the colonial power. District administration was the strongest unit of this system (Gaikwad, 1978). It has been further argued that the British design was itself based on the Mughal tradition of centralisation of power in the hands on one man making him the real ruler of the area. The latest government committee has emphasised the urgent need to reorganise administrative structures with radical departure from the feudal and colonial structure (Govt. of India, 1985).

Structural design coupled with strong resentment with and alienation from work and working conditions, accompanied by defensive behaviour and strong tendency to justify complacency with one's competence, disregard for guidance and help, and lack of concern for feedback and participation, pose serious obstacles to the implementation and management of anti-poverty pro-grammes. Therefore, it is no wonder that the stated goals of development have not been adequately achieved.

10

Summary and Conclusions

Indian planning has repeatedly stressed the need for raising standards of living and for creating new opportunities for the people. However, over the years there has been a concentration of wealth in the hands of a few and the gap between the rich and poor has tended to widen. The number of poor households increased during the period of intensive agricultural development. Therefore, from time to time attempts have been made to correct this situation by boosting agricultural and rural development. These policies have not been of much help to the poor. Land continues to be concentrated in the hands of a very small group of rich peasants and landlords with a large number of people either possessing little or no land. Despite declarations about helping the poor, the tendency has been to favour the wealthier residents. The trickle down theory has not worked and the poorest of the poor have remained untouched by the planning process.

The IRDP

The strategy of direct attack on poverty through the IRDP now covers all the development blocks in the country. Review studies show that the quality and the general impact of the IRDP has left much to be desired. There was a failure to assess the specific beneficiary oriented scheme against the availability of needed resources in the area resulting in widespread wastage.

Social Development

The performance in the field of education, health and other similar fields has also been very unsatisfactory. The constitutional directive for universal education, which should have been fulfilled by 1960, is still far off with nearly 64 per cent people illiterate. The rate of drop-out in primary schools is very high. More and more children are being forced to leave schools and become workers. The nutritional status of mother and child has been lagging far behind the required quality. Forest resources have been destroyed in several parts of the country thus creating an ecological imbalance affecting the lives of millions of people. The goal of providing safe drinking water to all by 1990 has still not been achieved. In fact, fewer people have access to clean and adequate water than ever before.

Unsatisfactory progress in social development has inevitably affected the lives of the people. Besides suffering from illiteracy, they are forced to live under unhealthy conditions, resulting in a high rate of infant mortality. The Seventh Plan has proposed new targets for improving the quality of life of the people. They have emphasised the need for the application of science and technology and for effective administration to achieve these targets. However, veiwed in the context of past experience, there are serious doubts about the satisfactory fulfilment of such targets.

The Parallel Economy

Over the years, the dismal development in priority areas seem to be related to the continuously expanding parallel economy and the emergence of the powerful factor of black money. Ironically, one of the important sources of such black money is expanding government expenditure itself. The great money power is used to create and finance pressure groups. It also provides political finance for elections and other such activities. Therefore, it is not possible to judge government policies by stated goals and priorities alone. What is more important is the actual performance in various developmental areas. It would be more instructive to analyse what governments actually do and why.

The Bureaucracy

The nature and role of the bureaucracy needs to be understood in the context of past development performance and the stated goals of development for improving the quality of life of the people. The bureaucracy has been important in India since British colonial days. Since then, it has greatly proliferated and has got entrenched in all walks of life. Analyses of development performance suggest that the bureaucracy is neither goal directed nor action oriented as far as alleviation of poverty, promotion of social equity and social development of people are concerned.

Administration by 'Fear and Awe'

The erstwhile ICS was known as the 'steel-frame' set up for protecting the interests of our colonial masters. They were not at all accountable to the people. They ruled by instilling fear and awe in them. The nationalist movement, therefore, perceived them as impediments to nation-building tasks. The ICS continued after independence and the last ICS officer retired only in 1980. In the meantime, the IAS took over the functions of the ICS. With tremendous proliferation, the bureaucracy has become increasingly and rigidly hierarchical in nature. Studies show that the values set by the British continued to guide the bureaucracy in India after independence and there was no radical departure in their behaviour from pre-independence norms. They were not positively oriented towards the elected political representatives at the ground level. They still practiced the colonial tactics of intimidating the people. Over the years, the bureaucracy failed to incorporate the desired changes in its structure and behavioural orientations.

Ascendancy of the IAS

Various committees and commissions have, from time to time, suggested the need for expanding the expert base of the bureaucracy. This has not been possible, and not only has it continued to be 'generalist' in nature (like the ICS) but over the years such cadres have emerged as the most powerful elements among the civil servants in the country. Administrative performance has been adversely affected due to increasing corruption. The legitimacy of both bureaucracy and political institutions has also greatly suffered as a result. Such conditions force the government to rely more and more on regulatory and 'law and order' bureaucracy. The ascendancy of the IAS needs to be viewed in this political context.

Bureaucratic Behaviour

It is no wonder, therefore, that despite repeated stress on participatory development and participatory administration, the old colonial 'steel-frame' and mentality seem to have been revived.

However, the tasks on the ground require experts, people's participation, high morale and motivation, harmonious relationship among different cadres of civil services and strong values and attitudes for working with the people. The emerging socio-economic and political situation, as briefly described above, has been marked by a development process of benefiting the rich more than the poor. Such a situation is not likely to shape the behaviour of the bureaucracy in the desired direction. The perceptual data collected from groups of senior bureaucrats, constituting the senior management at the central government level, confirmed this situation.

Perceptions of Senior Bureaucrats

Senior bureaucrats interviewed for the present study emphasised the need for people's participation but were at the same time highly sceptical of it. Most of them were not even aware of the ILO Convention 141 and the government policy for promoting the organisation of the poor. They, however, thought that such participation was no where in sight. They were sceptical of politicians and thought that political elements manipulate participatory forums for their own benefit. They apprehended that organisation of the rural workers, if promoted, would lead to law and order problems. Most of them were quite negative towards this policy and felt concerned about their 'neutrality' when conflicts between rural rich and poor emerged. A few of them, a very small minority, who favoured it suggested that civil servants should be re-oriented through training and educational programmes to become more sensitive and responsive to the needs of the poor.

Similarly, they were quite hostile to the idea of promoting staff participation in decision-making and management in government. They thought that it would further enhance indiscipline among them. A small minority, however, thought that staff participation would put a check on authoritarian tendencies among the senior bureaucrats and thus help loosen the present rigid administrative structure. However, all of them thought that the present system of administration was not conducive to promoting such participation.

Senior officials also perceived the need for developing subordinates' competence and equipping them for development tasks. They thought that the public officials in general were not prepared nd motivated for such tasks and that their morale was rather low.

They, however, did not perceive their own role in developing subordinates in this respect. They were clearly sceptical about the possibility of bringing about harmony and coordination among various development departments. They thought that vested interests entrenched in such departments do not allow such coordination to come about.

Word and Deed

The perceptual data thus brought out some important behavioural orientations obtaining at the senior level of the Indian bureaucracy. They seemed to show dislike and mistrust of politicians and trade unions. They talked about the need for developing subordinates but did practically nothing to achieve this task. They talked about the need for departmental coordination, people's participation and decentralisation, but again did little to change the situation.

The analysis of a sample of dominant views at the apex level of the Indian bureaucracy, therefore, revealed a split between the 'desirable' and what actually happens in practice—a split between word and deed. This split was one of the reasons for the poor functioning of the administration as a whole and lowered its credibility and responsiveness. Such a situation was likely to percolate down to lower levels of the bureaucracy with concomitant implications for development programmes.

Middle Level Officials

The respondents of the study with middle level public officials came from state and central government departments responsible for Agriculture, Water Supply, Animal Husbandary, Cooperatives, Irrigation, Afforestation, Education, Energy, Land Development, Food and Supply etc. They provided perceptual data regarding influence available to them at the workplace, working environment and work amenities, nature of their job and supervisory behaviour and practices. They also provided data on some aspects of their socio-economic outlook namely faith in people, sense of political efficacy, acceptance of current regime norms and liberal vs. conservative social attitude.

Information regarding some aspects of their development related behaviour was obtained with the help of specially designed development questionnaire. Factor analysis of the responses on this questionnaire yielded six constructs. They were identified as orientation for participation, tendency to justify performance, sense of complacency, 'association' orientation, orientation for seeking and giving coaching and feedback orientation. Various items were thus put together to compose six measures, one each for six development related bureaucratic orientations. Along with the measures of work related perceptions and socio-political outlook these revealed good reliability and validity. Multiple regression analysis identified the following important correlates of development related behavioural orientations and dimensions of work perception:

Participation Orientation: Faith in people and satisfying supervisory behaviour and practices for participation including tendency to promote people's participation and to get involved in participatory forums. Another important correlate of this orientation was the tendency to justify performance on the ground. Officers with a strong tendency to defend development performance (indirectly their own performance) were also high on the orientation supportive of participation.

Performance Justification: Performance justification seems to be accompanied by an orientation for association and the sense of complacency. Such officers, i.e., those with a strong tendency to justify and defend performance also expressed a high sense of political efficacy and strong dissatisfaction with their working and service conditions.

Sense of Complacency: The most powerful correlate of the sense of complacency was the tendency to justify and defend performance. It was also accompanied by a tendency for coaching; orientation supportive of participation; education. Length of service tended to weaken the sense of complacency and, therefore, enhanced the sence of vigilance. Involvement and interest in development work as well as professional and administrative experience and competence, therefore, emerged as its important negative correlate.

Coaching: Complacent officers also exhibited higher tendency to seek coaching. Similarly, conservative social outlook and satisfying supervisory behaviour also enhanced the coaching orientation. Interestingly, officers showing a tendency for feedback also appeared to show a greater tendency for coaching. The 'senior' officers, i.e., those with greater length of service also showed greater tendency for coaching.

'Association' Orientation: Officers with a greater sense performance justification and feedback orientations revealed a greater tendency for 'association'. However, the orientation supportive of participation lowered the tendency for 'association'.

Feedback Orientation: Both coaching and 'association' orientations seem to promote the tendency for feedback. Age and education also promoted a feedback orientation. Interestingly, job satisfaction greatly enhanced it and the length of service was a negative come late of this tendency. It appeared that, greater the length of service, lower was the tendency for seeking feedback on development performance and the concern for improving performance.

Perceived Influence at Work: Satisfactory working conditions followed by job satisfaction and satisfactory supervisory behaviour and practices greatly enhanced the perceived influence at work. Interestingly, officers exhibiting a critical attitude towards current political functioning felt much more deprived in terms of power and influence at work. In other words, supporters of the regime perceived much greater influence at work. However, this work behaviour appeared unrelated to development related orientations.

Perceived Amenities and Working Conditions: Perceived influence at work as well as satisfying supervisory behaviour greatly contributed to the satisfaction with perceived working conditions and work amenities. Interestingly, job satisfaction was unrelated to this perception. Officers having a greater sense of political efficacy and greater tendency to defend performance also showed greater dissatisfaction with their service and working conditions. Comparatively speaking, younger officers showed much greater dissatisfaction on this count.

Nature of Job—Job Satisfaction: The perceived influence at work emerged as the most important contributor to job satisfaction. It suggested that greater the influence perceived at work, greater was the perception of variety, challenge, meaningfulness etc., in the job. This provided a striking relationship between the context of work and the content of work. Comparatively younger officials perceived greater challenge and satisfaction in their jobs, suggesting a greater interest in development jobs. The orientation for feedback also made a substantial positive contribution to job satisfaction thus suggesting that perceived challenge in jobs was related to interest in development performance. Interestingly, the perceived nature of job and job satisfaction appeared to be unrelated to the socio-political outlook. Political behaviour, therefore, did not appear to be a factor in job satisfaction. The work itself, and its organisation as well as the concern for development, seemed to be the important factors in this respect.

Perceived Supervisory Behaviour: Here also the perceived influence at work was the most important factor contributing to perceptions of satisfactory supervisory behaviour/practices. It suggested that the middle level officers' perception of low formalisation and greater decentralisation at work also promoted perception of influence at work. Both factors were related to the nature of work organisation and style of senior management.

The longer serving officials seemed to be less satisfied with supervisory behaviour and practices. This reflected the importance of organisational variables relating to personnel policy where younger people are directly inducted over the already serving officials. It also suggested that such officials expected more respectful behaviour from newly inducted seniors and that such respectful relationship was not available. It is noteworthy that the respondents' age was not a factor. It is only the length of service which made the difference in their perception of supervisory behaviour. Bureaucratic orientations supportive of participation and coaching also emerged as positive factors in this respect. It suggested that supervisory behaviour supportive of participation and oriented to provide help through coaching etc., were perceived as more satisfactory. The findings suggested the importance of supervisory behaviour in promoting participatory management at the workplace in government.

Perceived Quality of Work Life (PQWL): The four dimensions of work situation exhibited high positive loadings on the first factor which was designated as the perceived quality of work-life (PQWL). The organisational factor of posting and transfer as indicated here by the position proximity to development (PPD) emerged as a clear negative factor in this respect. It suggested that the field officials, i.e., those posted near the implementation of development programmes, were significantly less satisfied with their quality of work-life. Another important finding in this respect was a clear relationship between people and political alienation and work alienation. Such middle level officials who showed a lack of faith in people as well as in themselves for influencing political matters, revealed much greater dissatisfaction with the quality of their work-life. Such officials felt alienated from people and political life on the one hand and from their work situation on the other.

Sense of Vigilance and PQWL: The sense of complacency emerged as a very important positive factor in the perceived quality of work-life suggesting that officials with a sense of satisfaction with their own competence were also satisfied with quality of their work-life. In other words, dissatisfaction with the quality of work-life in government organisations indicated a sense of vigilance among such officials. As vigilance is essential for ensuring the desired performance in development programmes, certain amount of dissatisfaction with the government work situation was, therefore, a positive factor in this respect.

There was an imperative need for providing more challenging job opportunities and better working conditions to government officials particularly for those placed in the field. This was also stressed by the senior officials. They clearly perceived these factors as very important for promoting morale and motivation among the officials. These findings also supported the importance of a proper placement policy.

Although there was a very significant relationship between political alienation and work alienation, politically efficacious and non-alienated field level officials seemed to be an exception to this rule. They felt highly dissatisfied with their working conditions and alienated from the workplace. Such officials appeared more interested in politics than work.

Placement and Bureaucratic Behaviour: In a rigidly hierarchical administrative structure, officials placed in the field enjoy comparatively lower status in the hierarchy. They are, however, placed much nearer to the implementation of development programmes on the ground. Such an administrative structure as defined by position proximity to development (PPD) seemed to shape important behavioural orientations as summarised below.

Superior–Subordinate Relationship: Length of service emerged as a separate factor in factor analysis. It seemed to indicate a sense of organisation status (OS). Interestingly, officials placed closer to the ground revealed higher OS. This factor appeared as a source of discord between directly inducted officials and other officers. The later category of middle level officers have a greater length of service to their credit and, therefore, carry a desire for better status in their organisation which is denied to them by the personnel policy. This in turn creates dissatisfaction with the superior-subordinate relationship at the ground level. Such discontent and strong feelings of work alienation are likely to affect their development related behaviour.

Political and Work Behaviour: As mentioned above, in the context of their work alienated field officials showed a much higher sense of political efficacy and acceptance of prevailing regime norms. They felt more at home in the prevailing political culture than the workplace. They also revealed a much greater tendency to justify development performance (i.e., their own performance). This finding reflected an important characteristic of political culture where leaders strongly tend to defend governmental performance, particularly in anti-poverty programmes. The field level officials also were more complacent about their preparedness and competence vis-a-vis development programmes. They did not care much for guidance, directives and coaching from senior officials. They also did not show interest in providing coaching to their own subordinates. Furthermore, they were less flexible and were inclined towards working and operating on their own. On the contrary, officers posted in secretariats appeared to show a much greater orientation for coaching, were less complacent and less oriented towards justifying performance than the middle level field officials who did not seem properly integrated in the bureaucratic hierarchy. Along with being structurally differentiated, they also appeared to be behaviourally different from those placed away from the field.

Some Concluding Remarks

Despite stated goals, the development performance over the years has left much to be desired. In actual practice, the important national goals, namely, growth; modernisation; self-reliance and social justice have been, if at all, achieved only partially. The bureaucracy responsible for implementing various development projects has got very widely proliferated, has acquired more powers and clout without becoming effective in achieving the development goals.

Senior bureaucrats seemed to be aware of such shortcomings in our development efforts. At the level of goals they saw the need for people's participation and participatory development programmes but in actual practice did little to implement such policies. They thought that the middle and junior levels of the bureaucracy were not adequately prepared for development tasks and that their morale, motivation and concern for development were low. However, in actual practice they did little to develop competence in their subordinates. Bureaucrats also showed mistrust of politicians and thought that they were not helpful in development efforts. They were also sceptical of, almost hostile to, trade unions.

The middle level officials posted in the field showed strong tendency for justifying ongoing development performance and had a sense of complacency about themselves. They did not like coaching from their seniors whereas their counterparts posted at secretariat and departmental headquarters were not averse to it. The former appeared to be politically more efficacious and nearer to the prevailing regime norms. However, at the same time they harboured a strong dissatisfaction with their working conditions and the quality of work-life. On the other hand, offcials posted at secretariats and away from the field felt much more satisfied in this respect. However, such satisfaction did not appear to be helpful in promoting a development orientations in them. On the other hand, officials who were more vigilant about development efforts, showed dissatisfaction with their quality of work-life. It appeared that officials having a critical approach to the functioning of the government and the political system were much more development oriented. Field level officials appeared more nearer the prevailing political system rather than to the system of bureaucracy of which they were a part.

Satisfactory supervisory behaviour and the tendency for receiving feedback appeared to be helpful in promoting participatory and performance orientations in government officials. Satisfactory nature of job and working conditions were also helpful in this respect. Those findings, therefore, suggested the need for widespread organisation redesign and reforms for promoting positive elements within the work structure and culture in order to inculcate development orientation in the bureaucracy.

Appendices

I Development Questionnaire (DEQ)*

Responses are obtained on a 4 point scale from 4: high/large extent/very good to 1: low/not at all/very poor; 4: very important to 1: not at all important/not required. The middle category (I do not know type) has not been included in the scale leaving two positive and two negative responses on a four point scale. The items are as follows:

Participation Orientation (NV–3)
23. It is often said that there is a need to generate/increase concern for developmental activities among the employees. What do you say about it?
19. Organisation of rural workers is considered important for their effective participation in developmental work. What is your opinion?
26. It is now accepted that there should be workers' participation in management. The Government of India has recently issued a new scheme for employee participation. It is being suggested by some people that there should be staff participation in government departments as well. How do you feel about it?

Participation Justification Orientation (NV–4)
30. To what extent is information about ongoing developmental programmes collected presently?
31. To what extent is information thus collected utilised for effective improvement in the ongoing developmental programmes?

Sense of Complacency (NV–6)
18. What is the general level of participation of people in development programmes?
20. Public administration is expanding. More and more people are joining government organisations. Tasks are becoming complex. In this context, how do you rate the preparedness and expertise of the staff, in general, to be able to handle their jobs?

22. We all know that employee involvement is very important for public administration. How do you assess such involvement presently?

Coaching–Dependence Orientation (NV–7)

16. It is said that one of the goals of development efforts is to increase self-reliance and internal capability among the rural poor themselves. How far has this been achieved?
21. How important is the role of the superior officers in this regard?

'Association' Orientation (NV–9)

27. Do staff associations and employee unions promote staff participation in government departments?
28. There are limiting as well facilitating environmental factors for developmental programmes. In general, to what extent do you think that such limiting and facilitating factors are taken into account in initiating and executing a programme?
33. There is now increasing talk of reducing red-tapism and increasing informality in government and in public administration. How do you assess the chances of success in efforts for minimising red-tapism and increasing efficiency in this regard?

Feedback Orientation (NV–10)

17. Many consider people's participation in development programmes to be important for the success of these programmes. What is your opinion?
29. It is generally emphasised that information about ongoing development projects/programmes is required on a continuing basis for improvement, if necessary, in these programmes from time to time. What is your opinion?

II   WORK QUESTIONNAIRE (WQ)

Responses are obtained on a 5 point scale. 5: very good/very high etc., to 1: very poor/very low etc. In some cases, this scale is reversed. The items are as follows:

Perceived Influence in Work-Life (V–12)

6. Employees have a curiosity to know what is happening in their organisation. Such information makes them feel important. How far are you able to get information about events in your organisation?

13. The organisation takes decisions many a time concerning you and your colleagues' welfare and interest. In what measure you are able to influence such decisions?

16. Sometimes you might feel that injustice is being done to you by the organisation. Is there any forum available in your organisation where you can get such a grievance redressed?

17. The organisation decides about the nature and schedule of work of the various categories of employees and they (employees) may or any not have participation in such decision-making. How is it in your organisation?

20. In work organisations many times people have to work together. They have to discuss with each other in order to come to decisions. Do people listen to each other in such a situation?

24. When people work together there can be a difference of opinion. Sometimes you may have an opinion quite contrary to that of your superior. How much freedom do you have to express such a difference of opinion?

Perceived Amenities at/in Work Place/Work-life (V–13)

2. Employees like to have good fringe benefits from the employers, for example, education of their children, medical facilities for their families etc. On the whole, how do you perceive such benefits in your employment?

3. Looking to the nature of your work, what do you think about your salary?

5. Drinking water is usually provided at the workplace by the organisation. How are facilities for drinking water in your organisation?

10. Employees are required to spend long hours at their work-places. Canteen and catering facilities are made available to them at appropriate hours. Are such facilities available in your organisation?

12. work organisations nowadays provide facilities for recreation

for their employees. How are recreation facilities available in your organisation?

21. Work organisations try to provide housing to their employees. How is the housing facility in your organisation?

Perceived Nature of Job (V–14)

1. At the place of work we may have the opportunity to learn some thing new, for example, skills in management, technical work etc. At some workplaces the organisation helps people to learn new jobs and skills.

9. Few people like to do the same thing again and again. They do not like to do repetitive work. How is the situation in your organisation? Do you get variety in your work?

11. People like to do a job in which there is a scope for them to use their skills and abilities. They perceive a challenge in such situations. How do you feel about your job?

14. People usually like to be on their own while doing their job. How much freedom do you have in doing your job without interferenc from your supervisors?

18. As several kinds of jobs are involved in a work organisation, some jobs may be perceived more significant than others. How do you see your job?

22. People like to do worthwhile jobs. What is the situation in your organisation? Are facilities available to you for working up to your own expectations?

Perceived Supervisory Behaviour/Practices (V–15)

4. In any work organisation, there are subordinates and superiors. How do you perceive the relationship between them in your organisation?

7. Employees do make suggestions about various things at the workplace. When you make a suggestion do your superior officers care for it?

8. We are happy when our good work is appreciated by those who count in the organisation. How much of such appreciation for good work is available in your organisation?

15. Do your superiors think that you are capable of doing a good job? What do they think of your work?

19. Sometimes employees feel that their superior officers do not plan properly and there are frequent changes in such plans. How is the planning in your organisation?

23. People need each others' support at the work organisation. How are your relationships with your superiors? Do you get support from them?

III SOCIO-POLITICAL OUTLOOK (PERSONALITY) GENERAL OPINION QUESTIONNAIRE (GOQ)

Response were obtained on a 5 point scale 5: strongly agree to 1: strongly disagree. The items are as follows:

Misanthropy
1. God has divided society into two classes, the rich and the poor.
2. Family planning is not likely to succeed in this country.
3. It is futile to hope that bad persons will be able to work with good persons.
5. Natural calamities can alone bring an end to social evils and personal quarrels.
6. We should not mix too much with others because it would produce mutual hatred.
7. Nationalisation of industries is bound to produce inefficiency and loss.
11. Persons belonging to different religious groups will always find it difficult to work together.
19. Elections have generally no meaning to me.

Sense of Political Powerlessness
13. Politics and government are so complicated that a citizen like me cannot really understand what is going on.
14. Irrespective of who you vote for things remain pretty much the same.
15. Nothing I can do seems to have any effect on what happens in politics.
18. It is no use worrying my head about public affairs; I cannot do anything about them anyhow.

Sense of Political Normlessness
12. Political parties are so big that an average member does not have much say in what goes on there.
16. Some people or groups have so much influence over the government that interests of the majority are ignored.

17. We talk of participation but common people like me have really no say in what the govenment does.

Conservative–Dogmatism
4. There is some supreme power above us and we should accept their decision without any reservation.
8. Military training must be compulsory for every citizen of India.
9. Most problems of our country are due to our low moral character.
10. For a happy life it is necessary to have faith in religion and God.

IV Varimax Rotated Factor Matrix (N = 119)

	Factor 1	Factor 2	Factor 3	Factor 4	Factor 5	Factor 6	Factor 7	Factor 8	Factor 9	Factor 10	Factor 11	Factor 12	Communality
V-1	-0.12776	0.01395	0.02441	-0.05337	0.61749	0.01138	0.16990	-0.24623	0.09960	-0.05221	-0.28070	-0.05703	0.058558
V-2	0.00898	0.84835	-0.23424	0.11144	0.04978	0.05436	0.07643	0.07297	-0.05490	0.02950	0.00268	0.03450	0.80876
V-3	0.10571	-0.08289	0.68002	-0.13215	-0.05086	-0.06509	-0.18750	-0.01867	0.03169	0.00262	-0.04914	0.10303	0.55432
V-4	0.08500	0.11092	-0.05109	-0.09871	0.13318	0.07139	-0.11900	0.19120	0.79168	0.02263	0.07561	0.08013	0.74408
V-5	-0.01016	0.90594	-0.09862	0.03449	0.04968	0.06088	-0.04637	0.01831	-0.02022	-0.11070	-0.01606	0.00364	0.85363
V-6	-0.14863	0.31193	-0.24258	-0.16785	0.22279	0.04870	-0.19091	0.29285	0.23528	0.14336	0.13699	0.31163	0.057245
V-7	0.00598	0.56890	0.39913	-0.04114	-0.13050	-0.06473	0.13133	-0.13277	0.42679	-0.01095	-0.11631	-0.07613	-0.74240
V-8	-0.04880	0.12992	-0.08672	-0.04853	-0.02091	0.80838	0.05932	0.00591	0.04358	0.02418	-0.01554	-0.00424	0.68936
V-9	-0.29856	-0.11440	-0.20230	0.02897	-0.10718	0.61671	-0.11648	0.12994	-0.13311	-0.09788	-0.02964	-0.25676	-0.66039
V-10	-0.45014	0.09214	-0.01481	0.04509	-0.36573	0.14801	0.14359	0.14456	-0.06163	0.34235	0.05060	-0.31996	0.63651
V-11	0.14217	0.22854	-0.45661	0.04858	-0.15745	0.12199	0.05463	0.37762	0.09313	-0.25343	0.07794	-0.11560	0.55372
V-12	0.84993	-0.01068	0.00402	0.01244	-0.09699	0.01328	-0.00576	0.08488	-0.06155	0.04161	0.10235	-0.07857	0.77253
V-13	0.48690	0.18700	0.04570	0.10405	-0.60542	-0.12390	0.04367	-0.07219	-0.09280	0.08088	0.09953	0.11039	0.71124
V-14	0.74159	-0.06210	0.06951	-0.02844	-0.01339	-0.13552	0.06194	-0.01501	0.04363	-0.00290	0.6697	0.22105	0.63733
V-15	0.81176	0.03281	0.06215	0.16949	0.00505	-0.11758	0.00306	0.11902	-0.03161	0.20048	0.12250	-0.04678	0.77903
V-16	0.27642	0.27465	-0.10071	-0.07846	0.09782	0.11264	-0.02318	0.29987	-0.61694	0.03553	0.09280	0.03426	0.67531
V-17	0.11671	-0.01481	0.44090	0.29434	-0.13574	0.25979	0.00921	0.24619	0.05614	-0.09312	0.17203	0.47339	0.70703
V-18	0.35118	-0.02030	-0.12533	0.23964	0.29312	-0.40229	0.41181	0.11204	-0.10343	-0.11212	-0.08118	-0.12593	0.67202
V-19	0.04561	0.08804	-0.01941	0.81229	-0.07605	0.03482	-0.17627	-0.10411	0.03105	0.05780	-0.04349	-0.02901	0.72597
V-20	-0.00576	0.03310	-0.19583	-0.08729	0.06433	-0.01894	0.81807	0.02437	-0.09793	-0.01899	0.10277	0.08359	0.74894
V-21	0.07962	0.03184	0.15231	0.05813	-0.07733	0.04400	0.02616	0.82905	0.01314	-0.04913	-0.05093	0.12612	0.75106
V-22	0.40187	0.00794	-0.14717	0.07119	0.23948	0.01441	0.21353	0.08920	-0.00542	0.61818	-0.17594	0.00327	0.071256
V-23	0.02860	-0.16216	0.60964	0.06949	0.07132	-0.14159	-0.06033	0.30190	0.02109	-0.19217	0.09083	-0.11208	0.58172
V-24	0.43600	0.12864	0.10464	0.40917	0.25080	0.21590	0.3302	-0.34515	0.11197	0.13780	-0.13452	0.13645	0.68336
V-25	0.26837	0.12423	0.04952	-0.15062	0.32782	0.34753	0.45052	-0.23206	0.24068	-0.13454	-0.04042	0.14513	0.69640
V-26	0.07356	0.00370	-0.09912	0.70705	0.14287	-0.16988	0.09779	0.24982	-0.14581	-0.01604	-0.04577	0.00383	0.66018
V-27	0.05511	-0.32095	-0.16749	-0.07914	-0.06247	0.02316	0.17268	-0.01587	0.06274	-0.16635	0.64976	-0.06687	0.63316
V-28	0.22958	0.22328	-0.02668	0.02024	0.11091	-0.00385	-0.32720	-0.10853	0.04008	-0.05347	0.62751	0.23456	0.68813
V-29	0.04913	0.00940	0.02414	-0.03360	0.07647	-0.10811	0.08137	0.06277	0.01100	-0.00454	0.02360	0.81567	0.69833
V-30	0.05790	0.21787	-0.01590	0.26382	0.53797	-0.23324	0.01574	-0.02470	0.08836	0.15556	0.28074	-0.07215	0.58140
V-31	0.22739	0.09756	0.01984	0.11126	0.60347	-0.13856	0.09723	0.06946	-0.22733	0.15840	0.34503	0.02149	0.66795
V-32	-0.06433	0.07413	-0.00396	-0.02364	0.03900	0.03139	0.14846	0.12784	-0.01373	-0.75398	-0.05671	0.01379	0.62319
V-33	0.06913	0.03698	0.35558	-0.12885	-0.03121	-0.04122	0.18891	0.10505	-0.08632	0.22868	0.55722	0.01886	0.56929

Bibliography

ADMINISTRATIVE REFORMS COMMISSION, INDIA. 1968: *Report of the Study Team on Machinery of the Government of India and its Procedure of Work*, Part II, Vol. I (Chairman: C.D. Deshmukh).

ADORNO, T.W. *et al.* 1950: *The Authoritarian Personality*, New York: Harper and Row.

AHUJA, KANTA and PRADEEP BHARGAVA, 1984: *Integrated Rural Development Programme: An Evaluation, Jaipur District*, Jaipur: Institute of Development Studies.

AHMED, B. 1971: 'Political Stratification of the Indian Electorate,' *Economic and Political Weekly*, Annual Number 6, pp. 252–258.

AHMED, S. 1986: *Role Stress and Perceived Quality of Work Life among Supervisors and Middle Managers*, Delhi: University of Delhi.

ALL INDIA CONGRESS COMMITTEE (I). 1979: *Congress Election Manifesto*, New Delhi: AICC(I).

—————. 1984: *Congress Election Manifesto*, New Delhi: AICC(I).

ATAL, YOGESH. 1969: 'Political Stratification of the Indian Electorate,' *Economic and Political Weekly*, Annual Number, pp. 171–78.

BANDHYOPADHYAY, D. 1985: 'An Evaluation of Policies and Programmes of the Alleviation of Rural Poverty in India,' in Islam Rizwanul (ed.), *Strategies for Alleviating Poverty in Rural Asia*, Bangkok: ILO-Asian Employment Programme (ARTEP), pp. 99 151.

—————. 1986: 'Land Reforms in India: An Analysis,' *Economic and Political Weekly*, XXI, A50-A56.

BANSAL, PREMLATA. 1974: *Administrative Development in India*, New Delhi: Sterling Publishers.

BANERJEE, SUMANTA. 1979: *Child Labour in India*, London: Anti-Slavery Society.

BHAMBHRI, C.P. 1972: *Bureaucracy and Politics in India*, Delhi: Vikas, Vol. 2.

—————. 1986: 'Bureaucracy in India,' in *A Survey of Research in Public Administration 1970–1979* (ICSSR), New Delhi: Concept, pp. 93–109.

BLAIR, HARRY W. 1980: 'Mrs. Gandhi's Emergency, the Indian Election of 1977, Pluralism and Marxism: Problems and Paradigms,' *Modern Asian Studies*, Vol. 14, No. 2, April, pp. 237–71.

BRAIBANTI, RALPH (ed.). 1966: *Asian Bureaucratic Systems Emergent from the British Imperial Tradition*, Durham, NC.

CENTRAL BANK OF INDIA, ECONOMIC INTELLIGENCE DEPARTMENT. 1983: *Integrated Rural Development in Chindwara District of Madhya Pradesh*, Bombay.

CENSUS OF INDIA,:1981 *Key Population Statistics based on 5% sample data*, Series I, Paper 2 of 1982, New Delhi: Registrar General of Census.

CHANDRA SHEKAR AND MOHAN DHARIA. 1969: Reported in *The Hindustan Times*, 5 December.

CHATURVEDI, H.R. 1977: *Bureaucracy and Local Community: Dynamics of Rural Development*, New Delhi: Allied Publishers.

DASHOLI GRAM SWARAJ MANDAL. (1982): *Hugging the Himalayas: The Chipko Experience*, Chamoli, Gharwal.

DASS, DURGA. 1969: *India From Curzon to Nehru and After*, London: Collins.

DESAI, A.R. (ed.). 1986: *Agrarian Struggles in India After Independence*, New Delhi: Oxford University Press.

ECONOMIC AND POLITICAL WEEKLY EDITORIAL, No. 27, 5 July, 1986.

FAO. 1980: *Review and Analysis of Agrarian Reform and Rural Development in the Developing Countries Since the Mid 1960s*, New York: WCARRD.

FACULTY OF MANAGEMENT STUDIES. 1985. *Community Participation and Management of Rural Development: National Seminar Report*, Delhi: University of Delhi.

FOURTH CENTRAL PAY COMMISSION. 1986: *Report*, New Delhi: Publications Division.

FULTON (LORD, CHAIRMAN). 1968: *The Civil Service: Report of the Committee, 1966–68*, London: Her Majesty's Stationery Office, Vol. 1.

GAIKWAD, V.R. 1978: 'Participation of Rural Institutions and Target Groups in Rural Development Programme Planning and Management,' Ahmedabad: IIM (mimeograph).

GERTH, H.H. and C.W. MILLS (eds.). 1948: *From Max Weber: Essays in Sociology*, London: Routledge and Kegan Paul.

GOPALAN, C. 1983: 'Nutrition at the Base,' *Seminar*, 282, pp. 19–24.

GOULD, D.J. and J.A. AMARO-REYES. 1983: 'The Effects of Corruption on Administrative Performance: Illustrations from Developing Countries,' *World Bank Staff Working Papers* No. 580, October.

GOVERNMENT OF INDIA, MINISTRY OF HOME AFFAIRS. 1964: *Report of the Committee on Prevention of Corruption* (Santhanam Report), New Delhi: Publications Division.

GOVERNMENT OF INDIA, MINISTRY OF FINANCE. 1971: *Direct Taxes Enquiry Committee Report*, New Delhi: Publications Division.

GOVERNMENT OF INDIA. 1985: *Report of the Committee to Review the Existing Administrative Arrangements for Rural Development and Poverty Alleviation Programmes*, New Delhi: Department of Rural Development.

GRIFFIN, KEITH. 1974: *The Political Economy of Agrarian Change: An Essay on Green Revolution*, Cambridge: Harvard University Press.

HALDIPUR, P.N. 1984: 'Bureaucracy's Response to New Challenges,' in T.N. Chaturvedi, S.P. Verma and S.K. Sharma (eds.), *Development Administration*, New Delhi: IIPA, pp. 97–109.

HARMAN, H.H. 1967: *Factor Analysis*, Chicago: University of Chicago Press.

HERZBERG, F. 1966: *Work and Nature of Man*, Cleveland: World Press.

————. 1968: 'One More Time: How do you Motivate Employees?,' *Harvard Business Review*, 46(1), pp. 53–62.

HIGGENBOTHAM, STANLEY J. 1975: *Cultures in Conflict: The Four Faces of Indian Bureaucracy*, New York: Columbia University Press.

HIRO, DILIP. 1976: *Inside India Today*, New York: Monthly Review Press.

HONADLE, GEORGE and INGLE MARCUS. 1976: *Project Management for Rural Equality*, Washington: USAID.

INDIA TODAY, March 15, 1984, pp. 126–29.

INDIAN INSTITUTE OF PUBLIC ADMINISTRATION. 1975: *Jawaharlal Nehru and Public Administration*, New Delhi: IIPA.

INTERNATIONAL LABOUR ORGANISATION. 1981: General Survey by the Committee of Experts on Application of Conventions and Recommendations, *Minimum Age*, Geneva
—————. 1982: Convention No. 141 in *International Labour Convention and Recommendations 1919–1981:* Geneva; ILO, pp. 15–24.
JAGJIVAN RAM. 1969: Reported in *The Hindustan Times*, 31 December.
JAIN, L.C. *et al*. 1985: *Grass Without Roots: Rural Development under Government Auspicies*, New Delhi: Sage Publications.
JAIN, S.C. 1983: *Impact Study of Integrated Rural Development Programme, Bardoli Taluk*, Gujarat: South Gujarat University.
JAIN, R.B. and P.N. CHAUDHURI. 1982: *Bureaucratic Values in Development*, New Delhi: Uppal Publishing House.
JANAK SINGH. 1985: *Times of India*, 14 October.
KALDOR, N. 1956: *Indian Tax Reform: Report of a Survey*, New Delhi: Ministry of Finance, Department of Economic Affairs.
KERLINGER, FRED N. and ELAZER J. PEDHAZUR. 1973: *Multiple Regression in Behavioural Research*, New York: Holt, Rinehart and Winston.
KERLINGER, FRED N. 1978: *Foundations of Behavioural Research*, Delhi: Surjeet Publications.
KRISHNA, A.C. KUTTY. 1984: 'A Case Study of IRDP in a Kerala Village,' *Indian Journal of Agricultural Economics*, October–December.
KRISHNA KUMAR. 1985: 'India's Primary Schools: The Funding of Desperate Needs,' *Monthly Commentary on Indian Economic Conditions*, 26 (9), pp. 69–74.
LELE, UMA and JOHN W. MELLOR. 1972: 'Jobs, Poverty and Green Revolution' *International Affairs*, XLVIII, January, 20–32.
Macauly Report (1884): Report of the Committee on Examination of Candidates for the Civil Service of East India Company (The report is reproduced as Appendix B of *Fulton Committee Report*, 1968).
MAN MOHAN SINGH. 1985: *Preface in Seventh Five Year Plan*, New Delhi; Planning Commission.
MATHUR, KULDIP. 1972: *Bureaucratic Response to Development (A Study of Block Development Officers in Rajasthan and Uttar Pradesh)*, New Delhi: National.
MATHUR, KULDEEP and ANIL GUPTA. 1982: *Action Research for Micro Level Planning: Self Appraisal*, New Delhi: IIPA.
MEHTA, PRAYAG. 1975: *Election Campaign: Anatomy of Mass Influence*, New Delhi: National.
—————. 1976: 'From Economism to Democratic Commitment: The Role of the Workers Participation,' *Vikalpa*, 1(4), pp. 39–46.
—————. 1976a: Efficacy and Alienation in the Imagery of Middle Managers and Workers Representatives,' *National Labour Institute Bulletin*, 2, pp. 302–308.
—————. 1977a: 'Employee Motivation and Work Satisfaction in a Public Enterprise,' *Vikalpa*, 2(1), pp. 559–73.
—————. 1977b: 'Participation, Efficacy and Politics,' *ICSSR Research Abstracts Quarterly*, Vol. VI (3 and 4), pp. 88–99.
—————. 1978: 'Objective and Subjective Factors in Employees' Satisfaction in Life and Work,' *Indian Journal of Industrial Relations*, 2 (13), pp. 433–44.

————. 1981: Political Behaviour. In *ICSSR Survey of Research in Psychology, 1971–76* (Part 2), New Delhi: Popular Prakashan.

————. 1982: *Manual for Personal Achievement, Social Achievement and Influence Motivation*, New Delhi: Participation and Development Centre.

————. 1985: 'Energizing Public Systems for Development,' Annual Lecture, 3 December, Faculty of Management: University of Delhi.

————. 1985a: 'Participation Management of Rural Development,' *The Administrator*, 30(1), pp. 73–90.

MEHTA, PRAYAG and MAHAVEER JAIN. 1979: 'Measuring Perceived Quality of Work-Life,' New Delhi: National Labour Institute (unpublished manuscript).

MELLOR JOHN W. 1976: *The New Economics of Growth: A Strategy for India and Developing World*, Ithaca: Cornell University Press.

MINISTRY OF EDUCATION. 1985: *Challenge of Education—A Policy Perspective*, New Delhi: Publications Division.

MINISTRY OF LABOUR. 1975: 'Scheme for Workers' Participation in Industry and Shop Floor and Plant Level,' *Gazette of India* (Extraordinary), Part I, Section I, 1 November.

————. 1977: 'Scheme of Workers' Participation in Management in Commercial and Service Organisations,' Resolution No. L-5602514/75-DK.I(B), 4 January.

————. 1983: 'Scheme for Employees' Participation in Management,' *Gazette of India* (Extraordinary), Part I, Section I, 30 September.

MISHRA, B.B. 1977: *The Bureaucracy in India: An Historical Analysis of Development up to 1947* New Delhi: Oxford University Press.

MURTHY, T.S. 1984: 'Planned Economic Change: The Components of Implementation,' in T.N. Chaturvedi, S.P. Verma and S.K. Sharma (eds.), *Development Administration*, New Delhi: IIPA, pp. 156–66.

MYRDAL, GUNNAR. 1968: *Asian Drama: An Enquiry into the Poverty of Nations,* New York: Twentieth Century Fund (three Volumes).

————. 1987: 'Address to Indian Parliament on April 22, 1958' reproduced in *IASSI Quarterly.*

NABARD. 1984: 'Study of Implementation of Integrated Rural Development Programme,' Bombay (memeograph).

NATIONAL INSTITUTE OF PUBLIC FINANCE AND POLICY. 1986: *Aspects of Black Economy in India*, New Delhi: NIPFP.

NEHRU, JAWAHARLAL. 1953: *Autobiography,* London: Methuen (Revised edition).

PENDSE, D.R. 1983: 'Deteriorating Situation,' *Seminar*, March.

PLANNING COMMISSION. 1978 *Draft Sixth Five Year Plan–1978–83,* New Delhi: Government of India.

————. 1980: *Sixth Five Year Plan—1980–85,* New Delhi: Government of India.

————. 1985: *Seventh Five Year Plan—1985–90,* New Delhi: Government of India.

————. 1985: *The Approach to Seventh Five Year Plan,* New Delhi: Government of India.

PUNJAB NATIONAL BANK. 1984: 'Impact of IRDP Advances in Rajasthan (An Evaluation Study),' New Delhi: PNB.

RAO, M.L. and PRAYAG MEHTA 1978: 'Measuring Implicit and Manifest Authoritarianism Development and Standardisation of Tools,' *Psychological Studies*, 23(1), pp. 10–18.

————. 1979: 'Communal Canker in Education: A Comparative Study of School and Family Environment,' *Indian Educational Review*, pp. 75–87.

RATH, NILANKAT. 1985: 'Garibi Hatao—Can IRDP do it,' *Economic and Political Weekly*, No. 26, pp. 238–46.

RUMMEL, R.J. 1968: *Applied Factor Analysis*, Evanston, Ill.: North Western University Press.

SHARMA, S. 1985: 'India Needs Water Use Policy,' *Times of India*, New Delhi, 30 April.

SHARMA, B.R. 1987: *Not by Bread Alone*, New Delhi: Sri Ram Centre for Industrial Relations and Human Resources.

SELBOURNE, DAVID. 1977: *An Eye to India: The Unmasking of a Tyranny*, Harmondsworth: Penguin.

SHILS, EDWARD. 1962: *Political Development in the New States*, The Hague: Mouton and Company.

SINGHI, N.K. 1974: *Bureaucracy, Positions and Persons: Role Structures Interactions and Value Orientations of Bureaucracy in Rajasthan*, New Delhi: Abhinav Publications.

STATE BANK OF BIKANER and JAIPUR. 1984: *Evaluation Study of the IRDP Beneficiaries in Bikaner District (Rajasthan)*, Jaipur: SBI.

STATE BANK OF HYDERABAD. 1983: *Monitoring-cum-Mid Term Evaluation of IRDP*, Hyderabad: SBH.

SUBRAMANIUM, C. quoted in Nirmal Mukarji 'Democracy and Development', *Future*, December 1985, pp. 6–13.

THIRD CENTRAL PAY COMMISSION. 1973: *Report*, New Delhi: Ministry of Finance, Government of India.

THOMPSON, VICTOR A. 1964: 'Administrative Objectives of Development Administration,' *Administrative Science Quarterly* No. 9.

TINBERGEN, JAN. 1976: *Reshaping the International Order: A Report to the Club of Rome*, New York: E. Dutton.

UNDP. 1979: *Rural Development Evaluation Study No. 2*, New York: UNDP.

UNITED NATIONS. 1980: *Public Administration Institutions and Practices in Integrated Rural Development Programme*, New York: UN.

UNITED NATIONS RESEARCH INSTITUTE FOR SOCIAL DEVELOPMENT.1974: *The Social and Economic Implications of Large Scale Introduction of New Varieties of Foodgrain: Summary of Conclusions of a Global Research Project*, Geneva: UNRISD.

WADE, ROBERT. 1985: 'The Market of Public Office. Why the Indian State is Not Better at Development,' *World Development*, 13(4), pp. 467–97.

WERTHEIM, F. 1969: 'Betting on the Strong', in A.R. Desai (ed.), *Rural Sociology in India*, Bombay: Popular Prakashan.

Index

schizophrenia, 55;
self interest, 48, 53, 54;
social base of, 62;
staff participation, 46, 47, 48, 49,
    59, 66, 106, 107, 157;
technical base of, 33, 34;
values expected of, 28, 29;
Weberian characteristics of, 31;
bureaucratic orientations,
  the constructs of, 75;
  development questionnaire (DEQ),
    70
      inter-correlations among items,
        76, 77;
      selected items, 165;
      variable description, 76
  the measures of, 85
      inter-correlations   among
        DRBO's, 88;
      reliability, 87;
      validity, 85;
      variance explained, 84, 85

Central Bank of India, 19
Census of India, 20, 21
Chandra Shekhar, 33
Chaturvedi, H.R., 32
Chaudhari, P.N., 30
child labour, 20, 21
coaching–dependence   orientation,
and
  age of officials, 100;
  bureaucratic leadership, 54, 150;
  complacency, 112, 159;
  concern for information, 112, 116;
  conservative–dogmatism, 100, 101,
    113, 159;
  the construct of, 81;
      career stagnation, 82;
      concern for development, 81,
        82;
      conservative-dogmatic outlook,
        82;
      helping behaviour, 82;
      hierarchical relationship, 82;
      job satisfaction, 81;
      position proximity to develop-
        ment (PPD), 82;

seniors' role in developing sub-
    ordinates, 81; staff partici-
    pation, 82
discontinuity in bureaucratic struc-
    ture, 149;
feedback orientation, 88, 100, 112,
    115, 116;
field officials' rejection of seniors'
    role in, 147, 149, 150;
help-giving, help-seeking beha-
    viour, 82, 112;
hierarchy in departments and
    secretariats, 82, 101, 112, 113, 149;
income of officials, 112;
influence at work, 100;
length of service, 100, 112, 160;
participation orientation, 112, 113;
political leadership, 150;
position proximity to development
    (PPD), 100, 112, 147, 149;
the regression analysis of, 111;
relationship oriented behaviour,
    101;
the scale of, 70, 166;
seniors' role in, 49, 50, 51, 55, 147,
    149, 150, 157, 158;
superior–subordinate relationship,
    113, 149;
supervisory behaviour, 100, 113,
    159;
work satisfaction, 101, 102
commercial banks, 33
community development, 15, 59
complacency, sense of, and
acceptance of regime norms, 100,
    146, 152;
achievement motivation, 146;
age of officials, 100, 109, 111;
amenities at work, 110;
coaching–dependence orientation,
    110, 111, 112, 159;
concern for poor, 149;
the construct of, 80
      achievement of internal capa-
        bility, 80;
      denial of conflict in pro-
        grammes, 80;
      involvement in administration,
        80, 159;